SITE PERSPECTIVES

SITE PERSPECTIVES

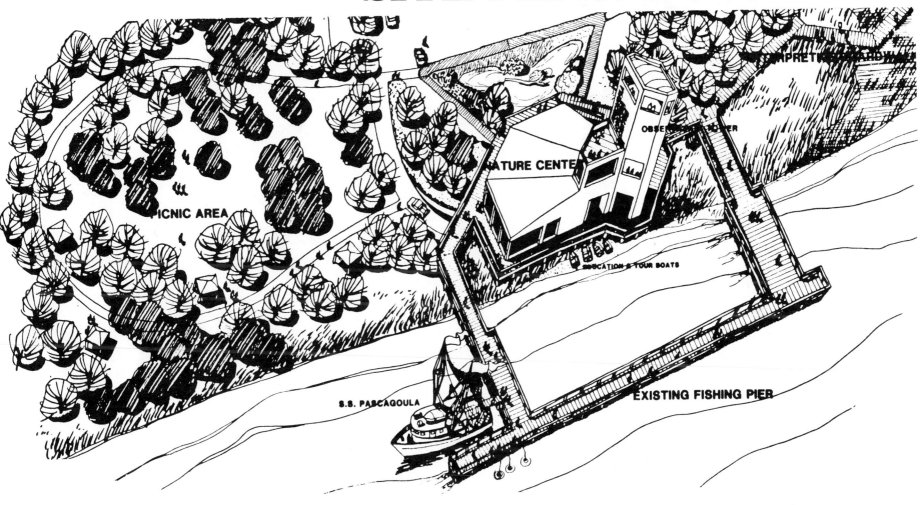

PICNIC AREA

NATURE CENTER

OBSERVATION TOWER

INTERPRETIVE BOARDWALK

EDUCATION & TOUR BOATS

S.S. PASCAGOULA

EXISTING FISHING PIER

L. Azeo Torre

Edited by William Lake Douglas
Foreword by William Turnbull

VAN NOSTRAND REINHOLD COMPANY
————————————————————————— New York

Copyright © 1986 by Van Nostrand Reinhold Company Inc.
Library of Congress Catalog Card Number 85-26390
ISBN 0-442-21848-6

Printed in the United States of America
Designed by Loudan Enterprises

Van Nostrand Reinhold Company Inc.
115 Fifth Avenue
New York, New York 10003

Van Nostrand Reinhold Company Limited
Molly Millars Lane
Wokingham, Berkshire RG11 2PY, England

Van Nostrand Reinhold
480 La Trobe Street
Melbourne, Victoria 3000, Australia

Macmillan of Canada
Division of Canada Publishing Corporation
164 Commander Boulevard
Agincourt, Ontario M1S 3C7, Canada

16 15 14 13 12 11 10 9 8 7 6 5 4 3 2 1

Library of Congress Cataloging-in-Publication Data
Main entry under title:
Site perspectives.
  Includes index.
  1. Landscape architectural drawing—Tilt-up technique.
2. Landscape architecture—United States—Designs and plans.
I. Torre, L. Azeo. II. Douglas, William Lake.
SB476.4.S58   1986   720'.28'4   85-26390
ISBN 0-442-21848-6

CONTENTS

All drawings were prepared by Cashio • Cochran • Torre/
Design Consortium, Ltd.

FOREWORD

by WILLIAM TURNBULL

In a time-oriented society, quality is often the first casualty if its achievement involves an excessive investment of hours. In the 1930s, time/motion studies and the accompanying attitudes of "quick and dirty" and "what's new is better" became popular. These societal attitudes are antithetical to quality design, especially in the realm of landscape architecture.

All of us, however, are products of—and are pressured by—our environments and the social forces that move them. Time concerns *are* a reality, and we must address them as such. Our traditional methods of communication, drawings and sketches, must be reinterpreted in the economic struggle of everyday life. Big firms, both in architecture and landscape architecture, are increasingly turning to the computer to speed up the rendering process. What is needed is additional help in the design process. The computer can model topography for us, but it cannot design to accommodate the ecosystems and landscapes associated with it. Our traditional and laborious descriptive methods, renderings, axonometric drawings and the like are self-limiting because of the costs and time necessary to produce such studies.

Site Perspectives demonstrates how to alleviate these problems, enabling designers to envisage their landscapes using a quick and easy methodology. As a tool, its success will lie in the hands of its user: its promise however is for clearer explorations of the landscape, more informative discussions with the user-client, and in the end, better solutions and better landscapes for us all to inhabit and enjoy.

William Turnbull

GRAPHIC COMMUNICATION
for SITE DESIGNERS

Drawing has historically been used as the universal language of visual communication. It has, in fact, been the vehicle for translating conceptual thought into graphic reality. It is also the most convenient means by which a designer can delineate a design concept and manipulate it through a personal design process. Drawing is a mechanical response to the conceptual nature of design thought. In this book, we demonstrate our own method of presentation drawing, which includes traditional methods (plans, sections, and perspectives) as well as a new approach to site illustration, a technique we call *tilt-up*.

This technique, a free-form combination of aerial, axonometric, isometric, and one-point perspective drawings, is a simple means by which a design concept can be illustrated, studied, and presented effectively. The three-dimensional aspect of the tilt-up drawing is achieved by "peeling back" the facades of buildings or site elements and tilting them into various vertical planes to expose all elements of the design for review and study. Tilt-up drawings offer a greater sense of scale and detail than traditional plan techniques, which often result in flat, two-dimensional presentations that lack comparable detail and information. This tilting effect is, for the most part, devoid of formula and technique, thus allowing for more free-form design solutions. The lines to which the three-dimensional elements vanish do not have to be derived from fixed stations—the object is to create a feeling of three-dimensionality within the drawing, rather than to focus on a level of mechanical accuracy. Through this intuitive approach to drawing, the process, with practice, becomes a fast, efficient way to design in three rather than two dimensions.

The approach does not radically differ from other approaches to drawing. Like the drawings of masters from Leonardo da Vinci to Jacobi, this new rendering style is a method for delineating design concepts within the currently established language of graphic communication. The tilt-up drawing process differs from traditional approaches in the amount of freedom or flexibility it allows in the presentation format, and the speed with which a simple or complicated site can be described graphically and understood visually.

The tilt-up technique, as both a design aid and a presentation tool, is not new. Although the approach developed because of the need to communicate effectively and efficiently with non-design-oriented clients and was independent of any previous technique, it is similar to the presentation styles employed by landscape architects in the 1940s and 1950s. The difference between the two approaches is evident in the final products. In the earlier format, plant forms were stylized almost to the point of abstraction, whereas, using the tilt-up technique, cartoonlike renderings that depict less abstract versions of plant forms and provide for realistic spatial interpretations are produced.

Many of these drawings are not necessarily finished presentation drawings. The tilt-up technique creates a fluid, graphic language by which the drawing becomes a working tool itself—an efficient means to creating an effective final presentation.

Tilt-ups offer many advantages: they are nontechnical in format and construction, quickly prepared, and "viewer friendly." The ability to use the results as a basis for larger presentations, as well as the opportunity to use the technique for personal notation and communication with other designers, is inherent in this approach.

As we enter the age of computer drawing and the application of advanced technology to the design profession, it is even more important to continue to draw. While the computer offers a tremendous wealth of opportunities to store and retrieve data, it can not substitute for the physical realization of the intuitive design process.

All designers should draw. Drawing enables the designer to use the mechanical relationship between mind and hand in order to study all aspects of a design and to understand more clearly the scale, space, and texture created by a design. Moreover, a tremendous amount of design personality can be developed through drawing skills. The tilt-up approach gives the designer a realistic and workable drawing technique that allows for an economical yet comprehensive level of graphic communication and ultimately, a higher level of design accomplishment.

By studying the examples in this book, it will be obvious that there is no scale at which the tilt-up technique does not work. Representative drawings range in final format from six inches to eighteen feet in length, and the approach for any size project remains the same: the presentation should evolve from a determination of the major theme to a drawing that features the established theme. The drawing itself, therefore, creates a focus for the elements within it. A uniform line weight is used to give a consistent outline to forms and shapes, which can be further articulated with color (we use markers, but any medium will work). If this line weight is not maintained, the strength of the colors may "wash out" some of the outline, thus requiring the designer to redraw or darken these elements.

The tilt-up technique allows the designer to move from what has traditionally been called the "schematic" or preliminary design phase to what we call a "thematic" design phase, which offers specific solutions to the particular design problems at hand. The three-dimensionalization allows for closer study and design clarity and subsequently a higher level of conceptual articulation. Tilt-ups combine conventional plan and elevation sketches, to facilitate the study of floor and vertical plans in one single drawing. This not only creates a "spatial volume" within the drawing itself, but saves time and creates a drawing that is more easily understood by a non-design-oriented audience. As each plane is studied, manipulated, brought into focus, juxtaposed against other components, and then finally delineated, the designer and client become acutely aware of all components of the drawing and with all the parts of the design.

These drawings can be photographed and reproduced, in whole or in part, which allows for a tremendous amount of flexibility in presentation technique. When reduced photographically, the image becomes "tighter" and appropriate for reports, books, and small formats. When enlarged, the line quality becomes grainy and thick, giving an "informal," abstract quality to the sketch.

Tilt-up drawings used for public meetings and interactions with clients have proven successful because of the ease with which the layman can visualize the proposed design issues. By studying design proposals in this format, the designer is allowed then to be less protective of the finalized design drawing and more free to manipulate the design. The client is not intimidated by frozen, hard lines and is more willing to "brainstorm" with the designer.

The overlay process is another critical factor in our design process. The incremental and flexible buildup of design elements—quickly sketched, transposed, corrected, and pasted—advances the design process without requiring redrawing. The time saved by eliminating this redundancy is translated into productive design time, allowing the designer to increase the level of quality and often the quantity of the final package. Other designers will find, as we have, that this technique eliminates the hesitation to commit to a design scheme and gives greater latitude and freedom to the designer.

We have found that by using the tilt-up technique and overlay approach to design, our designs have improved, our productivity has increased, and we are able to communicate more easily with non-design-oriented clients.

It is not the purpose of this book to suggest an elimination of traditional techniques of design delineation, but rather to propose a pragmatic, day-to-day working technique by which the designer can use drawing as a major design tool. It is our feeling that, "if you can't see it, you can't design it" and, therefore, if drawings are not clear and readable, or if it appears as if a design purpose has not been diligently pursued, the final product will be confused and disorganized. Using these techniques, the designer will also achieve a higher level of enjoyment in the schematic and design-development phases of the overall design process. These approaches remain open to new thought and interpretation. Enjoying the design process will lead to both a better design and a better experience for all involved. We hope that this book will be kept by the side at the desk of designers and that the reward will be fulfilling.

BASIC TILT-UP TECHNIQUE
The Rough Sketch
Time Required: 2 hours

Lay out the site plan and secure it to the drafting table. Assemble your drawing equipment: standard yellow tracing paper, Pentel pens, and triangles. Decide which design elements are most important to depict. Using a yellow tracing paper overlay, make preliminary sketches to evaluate the position of elements and presentation requirements. Draw trees and other vertical elements perpendicular with the lower edge of the paper, making them conform to the plan scale (figs. 1 and 2).

When necessary, make several overlays to study different positions of buildings and plants and the composition of existing and proposed features. Design concepts can be effectively and efficiently studied at this stage (figs. 3 and 4).

Begin the sketch at the lower left corner of the paper and work clockwise if right-handed. Left-handed individuals should reverse the process. This prevents the designer from working on top of previously finished components of the drawing, and thus avoids the smearing or soiling of these areas. Limit tree representations to four or five basic shapes: deciduous trees, small trees, evergreens, and the like. Strive to capture the character of indigenous plant material. Shadows can be added to the ground plane as trees are drawn (figs. 5 and 6).

Step back from the drawing periodically (even stand above it or tack it on the wall) to get an idea of how the drawing looks (fig. 7).

1

2

3

4

5

6

7

The Final Sketch
Time Required: 3 hours

When the rough sketch is complete, cover it with a large sheet of yellow trace (or vellum) and begin the process of redrawing to create the final sketch. Work counterclockwise, from lower right to lower left (figs. 8–13). The drawing process should go quickly and the final drawing should have a loose, informal character.

8

9

10

11

12

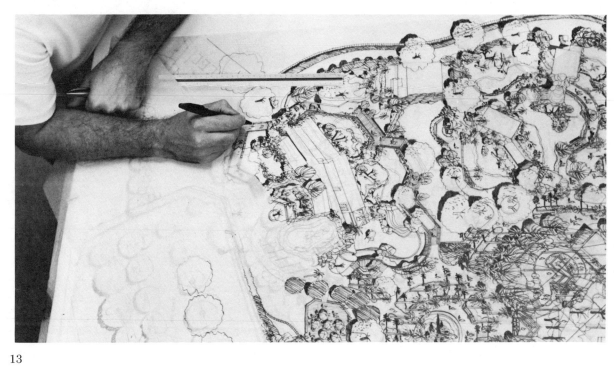

13

Check that all shadows are in place; add people and other details to give life to the drawing. If necessary, add dry-transfer lettering (such as Kroy or Presstype) to label significant features. When all information is on the drawing, run print (high-contrast print paper takes marker better than regular print paper). Assemble the office staff and collectively color. For final drawing, see page 41 (Tampa's Lowry Park Zoo). See also figures 14–16.

14

15

16

PROJECTS

RECREATION

Project: Audubon Park and Zoological Garden
Client: Audubon Park Commission, City of New Orleans
Location: New Orleans
Date: 1974–present
Presentation: Blackline drawings, colored poster
Budget: $20 million
Status: Complete

    This project consisted of a series of separate developments that could not
be effectively illustrated using traditional plan methods. Traditionally, zoos
end up looking like squares and boxes with wiggly forms connecting them,
and one is not easily able to ascertain the locations of various facilities and
structures that make up the exhibit. This is one of the first projects for which
we used the tilt-up technique to illustrate individual segments of the project.
The aerial view, drawn after designs were developed for the whole site, gave a
comprehensive view of the entire project. In specific projects such as the
Audubon Batture and Odenheimer Aquarium, we were able to delineate
clearly each part and each phase leading to the finished project. This view was
reproduced as a color poster (24 by 36 inches). It is used in the zoo as an
orientation map and is sold at the "Zootique." It is also an effective tool for
marketing our professional services as zoo designers.

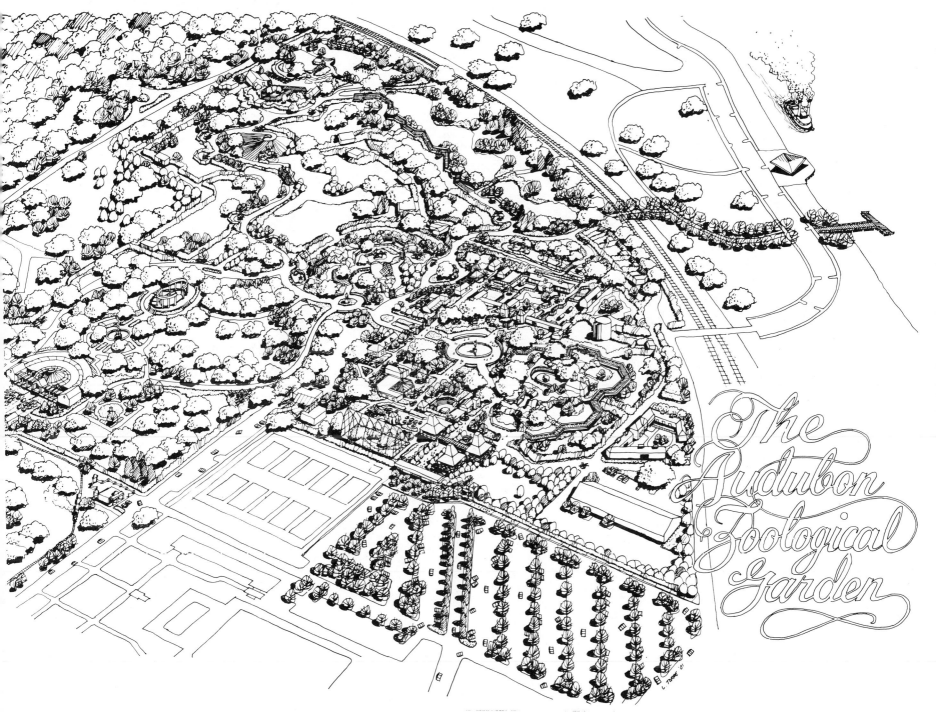

The Audubon Zoological Garden

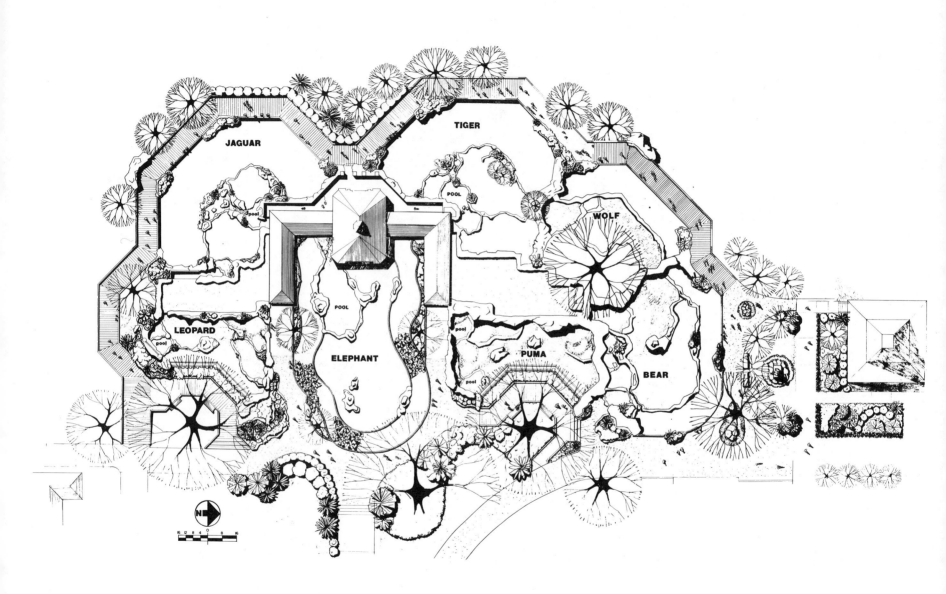

JAGUAR

TIGER

WOLF

LEOPARD

pool

POOL

ELEPHANT

pool

PUMA

pool

BEAR

N

16 12 8 4 0 8 16

RING TAILED LEMUR

TREE SHREW

SIMANG GIBBON

BUSH BABY

LORIS

OWL MONKEY

SQUIRREL MONKEY

LOWLAND GORILLA

COLOBUS MONKEY

SPIDER MONKEY

MARMOSET

SPECTACLED LANGUR

MOOR MACAQUE

DIANA MONKEY

MANGABEY MONKEY

GELADAS BABOON

ORANGUTAN

16 12 8 4 0 8 16

NEW ORLEANS

WORLD OF PRIMATES

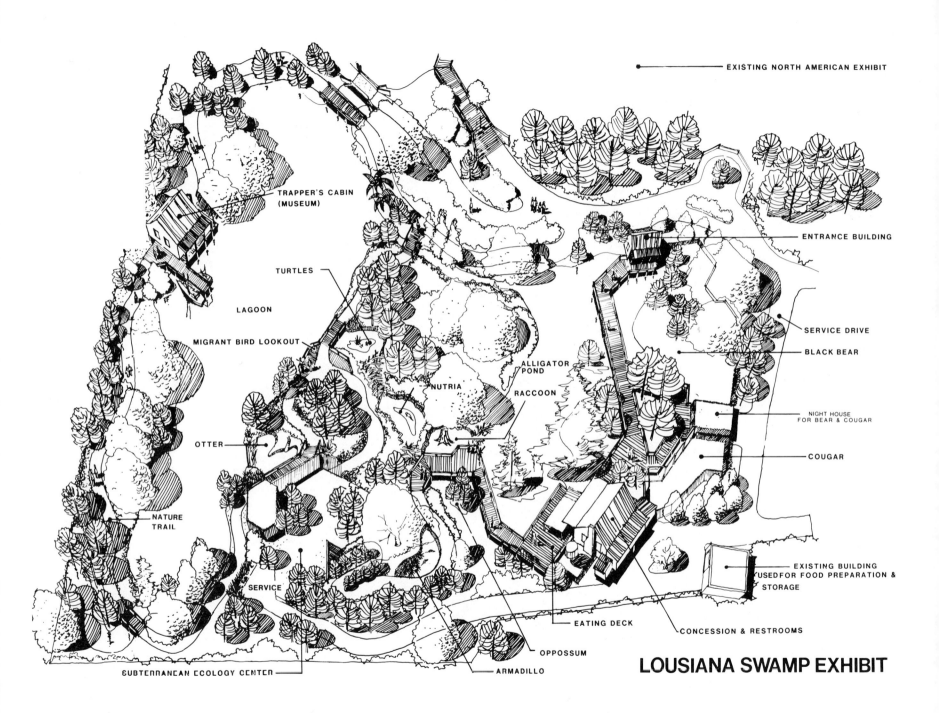

EXISTING NORTH AMERICAN EXHIBIT

TRAPPER'S CABIN (MUSEUM)

ENTRANCE BUILDING

TURTLES

LAGOON

MIGRANT BIRD LOOKOUT

SERVICE DRIVE

BLACK BEAR

ALLIGATOR POND

NUTRIA

RACCOON

NIGHT HOUSE FOR BEAR & COUGAR

OTTER

COUGAR

NATURE TRAIL

EXISTING BUILDING USED FOR FOOD PREPARATION & STORAGE

SERVICE

EATING DECK

CONCESSION & RESTROOMS

SUBTERRANEAN ECOLOGY CENTER

OPPOSSUM

ARMADILLO

LOUSIANA SWAMP EXHIBIT

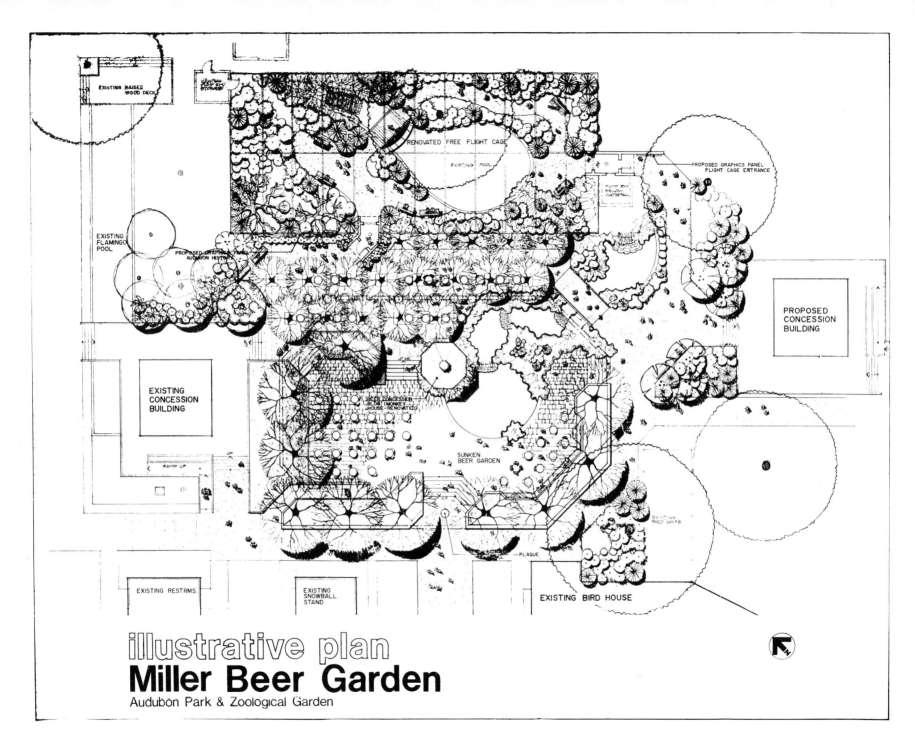

EXISTING RAISED WOOD DECK

RENOVATED FREE FLIGHT CAGE

EXISTING POOL

PROPOSED GRAPHICS PANEL
FLIGHT CAGE ENTRANCE

PUMP RM
BELOW
WATERFALL

EXISTING
FLAMINGO
POOL

PROPOSED GRAPHICS PANEL
AUDUBON HISTORY

PROPOSED CONCESSION
BUILDING

EXISTING
CONCESSION
BUILDING

BEER CONCESSION
BLDG (MONKEY
HOUSE-RENOVATED)

RAMP UP

UP

SUNKEN
BEER GARDEN

EXISTING
BIRD CAGE

PLAQUE

EXISTING RESTRMS.

EXISTING
SNOWBALL
STAND

EXISTING BIRD HOUSE

illustrative plan
Miller Beer Garden
Audubon Park & Zoological Garden

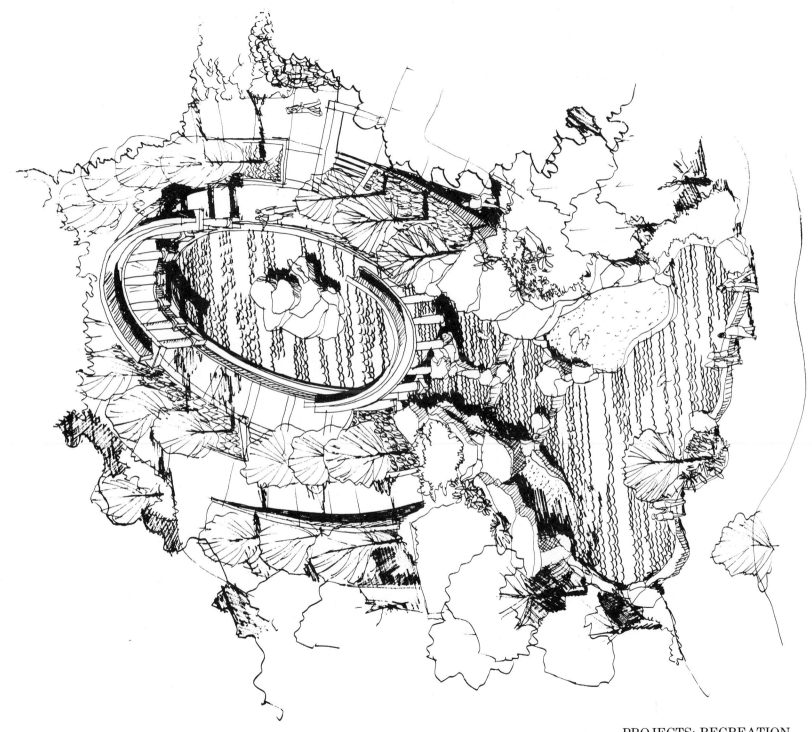

SEA LION EXHIBIT

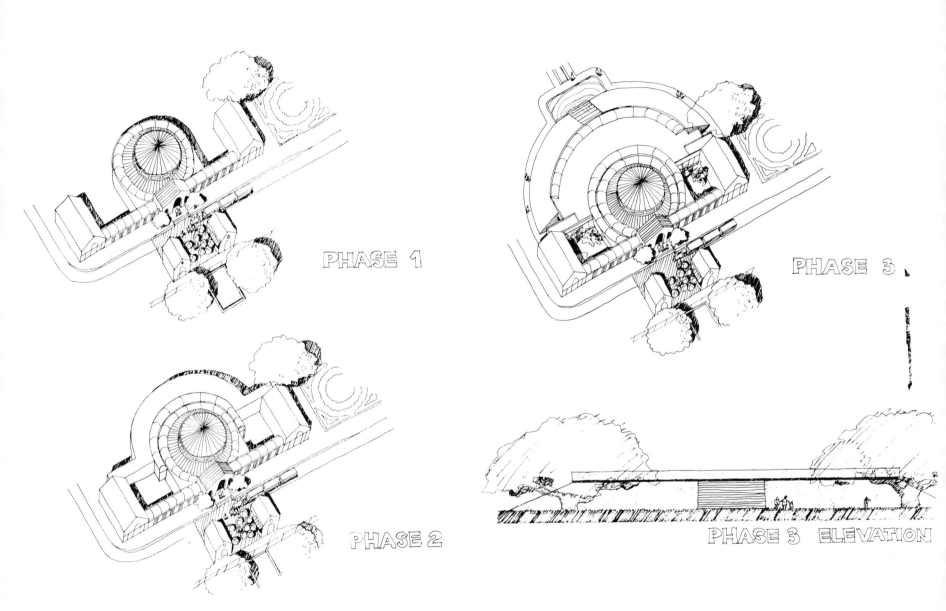

PHASE 1

PHASE 3

PHASE 2

PHASE 3 ELEVATION

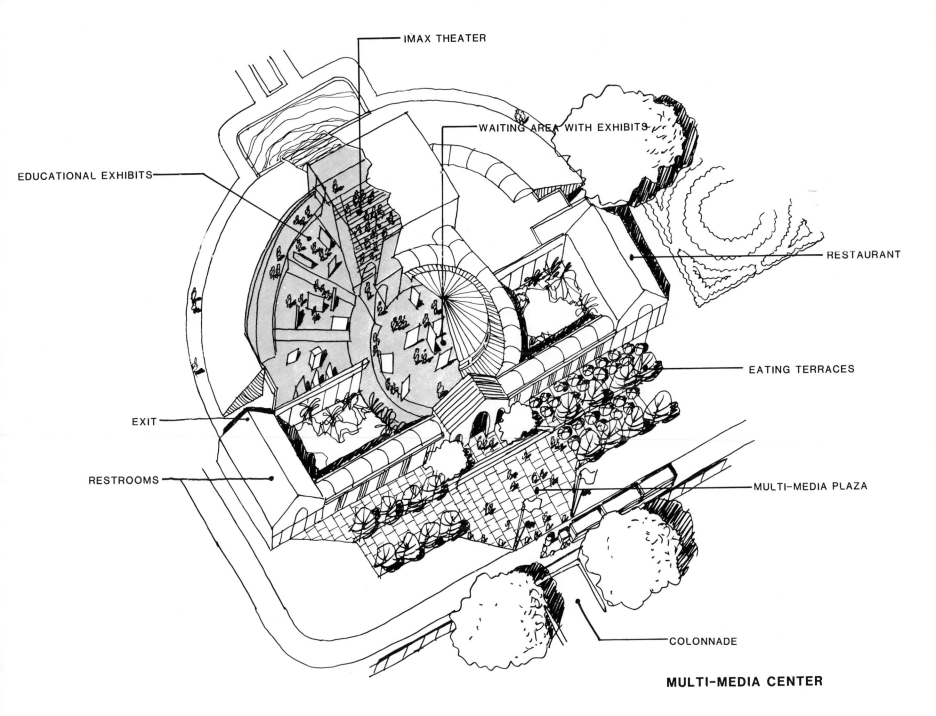

IMAX THEATER

WAITING AREA WITH EXHIBITS

EDUCATIONAL EXHIBITS

RESTAURANT

EATING TERRACES

EXIT

RESTROOMS

MULTI-MEDIA PLAZA

COLONNADE

MULTI-MEDIA CENTER

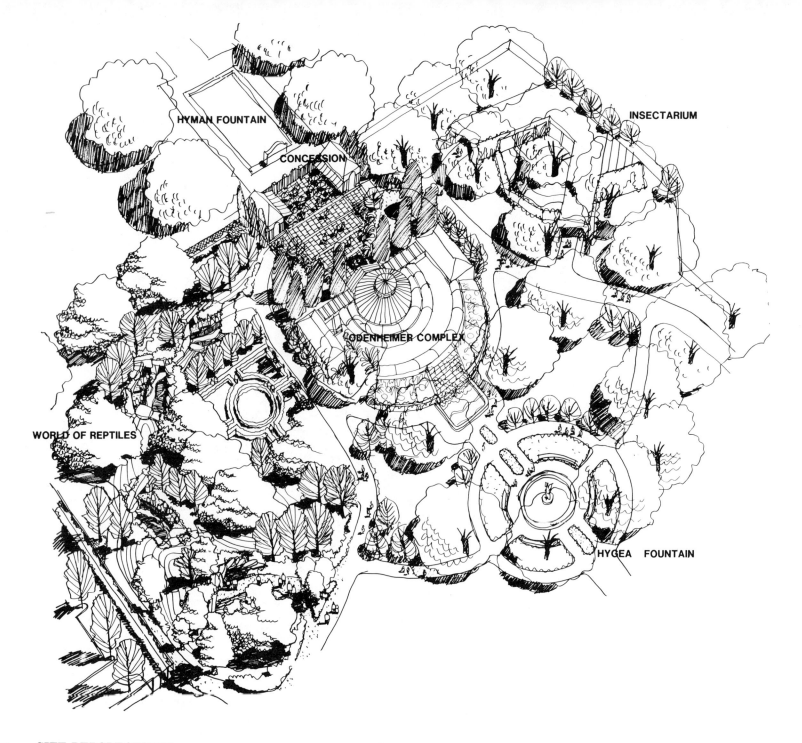

HYMAN FOUNTAIN

CONCESSION

INSECTARIUM

ODENHEIMER COMPLEX

WORLD OF REPTILES

HYGEA FOUNTAIN

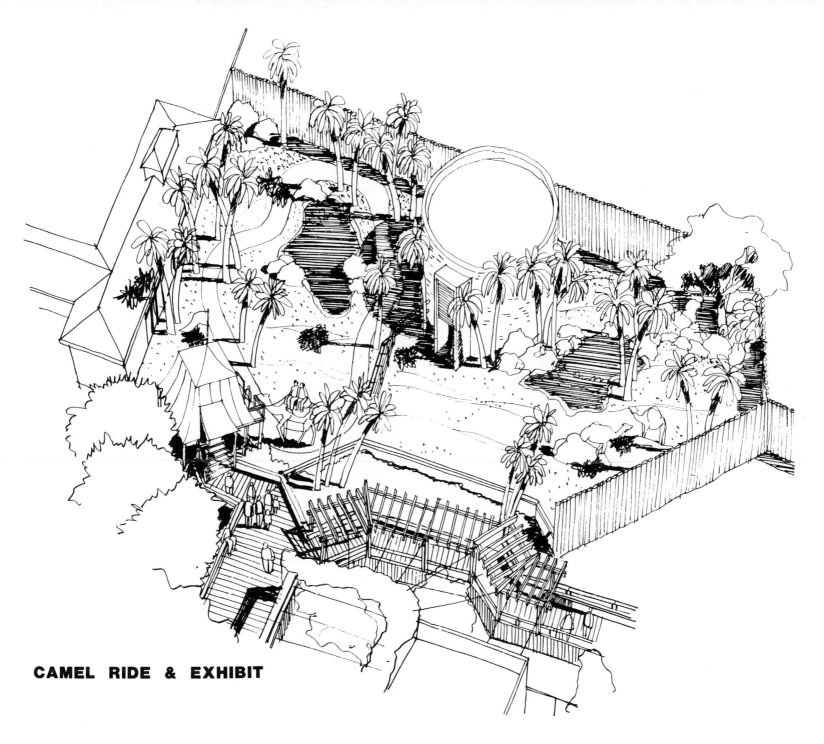

CAMEL RIDE & EXHIBIT

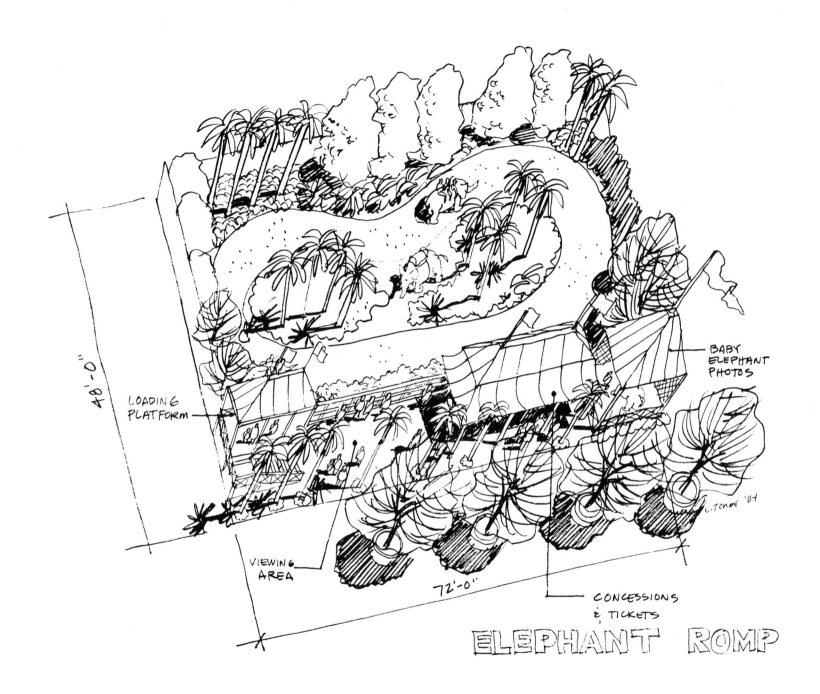

48'-0"

LOADING
PLATFORM

BABY
ELEPHANT
PHOTOS

VIEWING
AREA

72'-0"

CONCESSIONS
& TICKETS

ELEPHANT ROMP

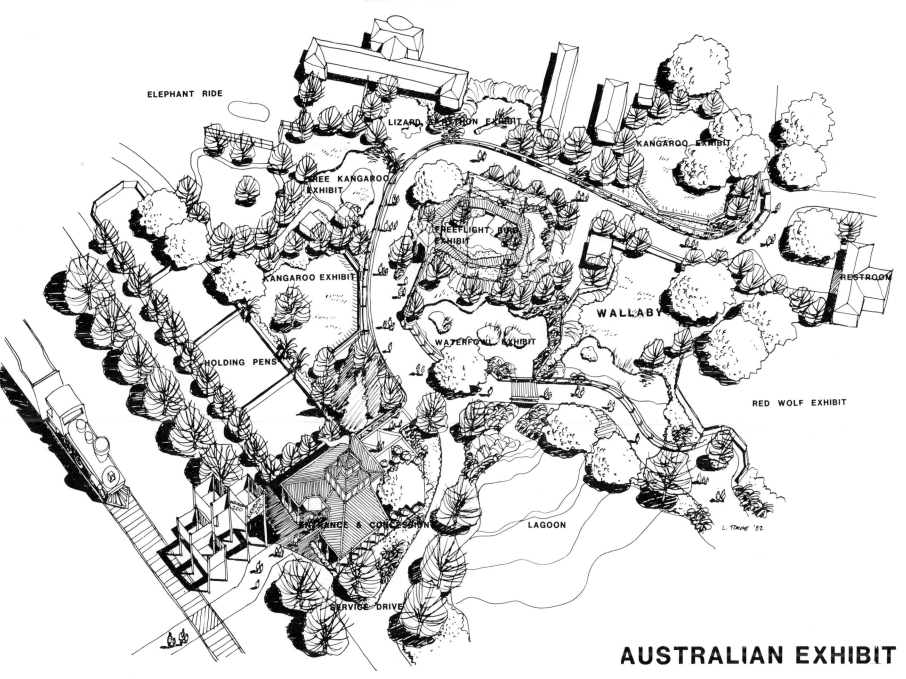

CHILDRENS VILLAGE

ELEPHANT RIDE

LIZARD & PYTHON EXHIBIT

KANGAROO EXHIBIT

TREE KANGAROO EXHIBIT

FREEFLIGHT BIRD EXHIBIT

KANGAROO EXHIBIT

RESTROOM

WALLABY

WATERFOWL EXHIBIT

HOLDING PENS

RED WOLF EXHIBIT

ENTRANCE & CONCESSION

LAGOON

L. TORRE '82

SERVICE DRIVE

AUSTRALIAN EXHIBIT

Project: Bayou Segnette State Park
Client: State of Louisiana
Location: Jefferson Parish, Louisiana
Date: 1982–84
Presentation: Sketches for report format; blackline prints
Budget: $10 million
Status: Under construction

Bayou Segnette State Park is a 600-acre state park development. We used the tilt-up technique to show how various components—such as the boat launch facility, day-use area, group camp, cabin clusters, and the park center complex—fit into the wooded environment. Architectural character, selective clearing, and controlling views from the structures are clearly illustrated in the drawings. The style of the drawings reinforces our approach to state park design, which advocates the design of recreational facilities with an obligation to present local environmental, cultural, and historic aspects of the region in its site plans, architecture, and furnishings. The building designs are metaphors for native structures with broad overhangs, cupolas, standing seam roofs, and the like.

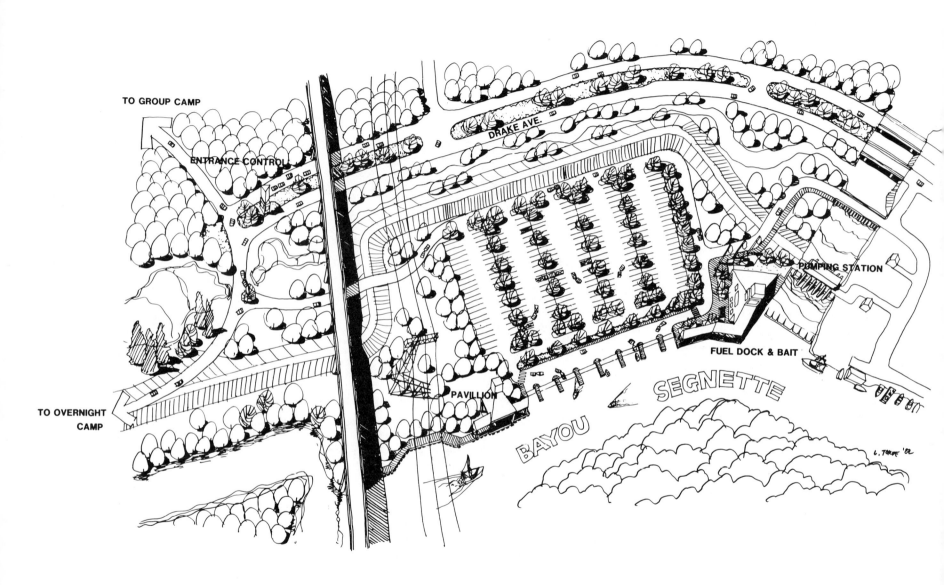

TO GROUP CAMP

ENTRANCE CONTROL

DRAKE AVE.

TO OVERNIGHT
CAMP

PAVILLION

PUMPING STATION

FUEL DOCK & BAIT

BAYOU SEGNETTE

L. TORRE '82

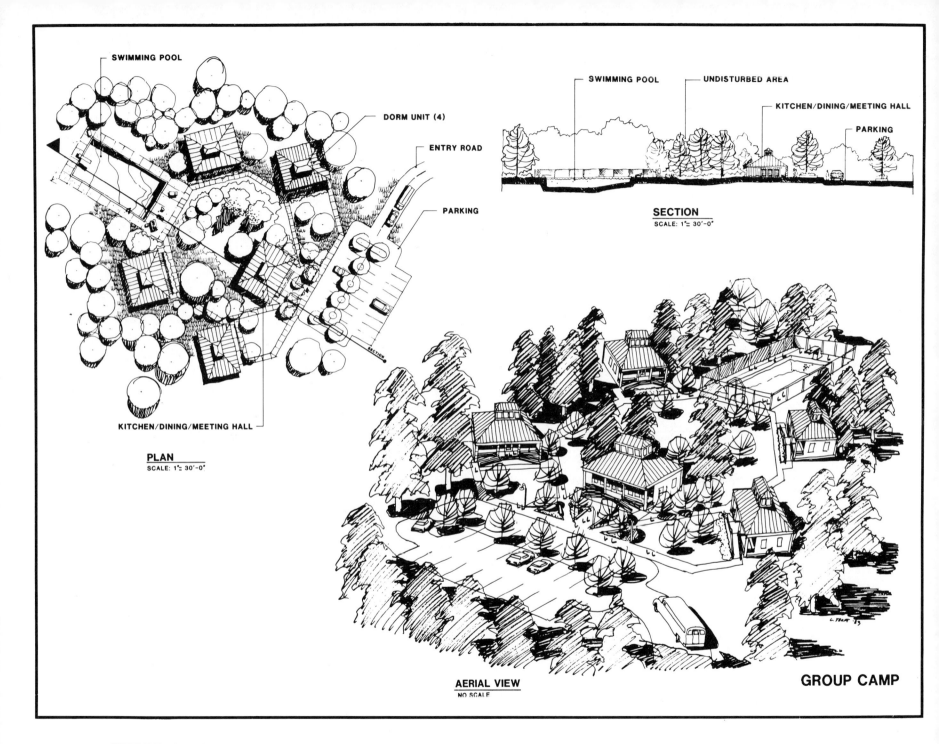

SWIMMING POOL

DORM UNIT (4)

ENTRY ROAD

PARKING

KITCHEN/DINING/MEETING HALL

PLAN
SCALE: 1"≃ 30'-0"

SWIMMING POOL

UNDISTURBED AREA

KITCHEN/DINING/MEETING HALL

PARKING

SECTION
SCALE: 1"≃ 30'-0"

AERIAL VIEW
NO SCALE

GROUP CAMP

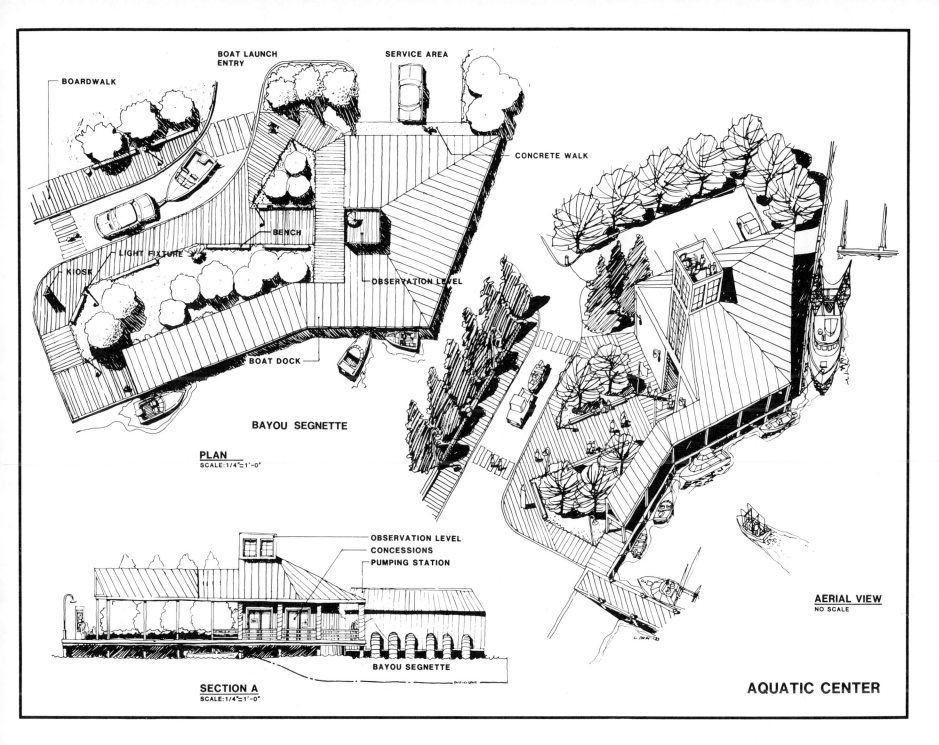

BOARDWALK

BOAT LAUNCH
ENTRY

SERVICE AREA

CONCRETE WALK

BENCH

LIGHT FIXTURE

KIOSK

OBSERVATION LEVEL

BOAT DOCK

BAYOU SEGNETTE

PLAN
SCALE: 1/4"=1'-0"

OBSERVATION LEVEL
CONCESSIONS
PUMPING STATION

BAYOU SEGNETTE

SECTION A
SCALE: 1/4"=1'-0"

AERIAL VIEW
NO SCALE

AQUATIC CENTER

Project: Small Playgrounds
Client: City of New Orleans
Location: New Orleans
Date: 1983–84
Presentation: Blackline prints with marker
Budget: $5 million
Status: Complete

Public meetings are essential to the design process for any municipal playground, park, or plaza. The success or failure of the project will depend on the ability of the public to understand all of the aspects and ramifications of the final design. In this series of projects, we found the tilt-ups to be very effective, because they can depict building facades. The public could, therefore, pinpoint neighborhood landmarks and structures and thus understand the placement of various design elements and how new features would affect access routes, views, and the like. A series of meetings was held for these projects, which revealed a positive response to the drawings, thus making them highly useful design vehicles. The realism of the tilt-up technique allows the participants in the public planning process to envision themselves within the proposed development.

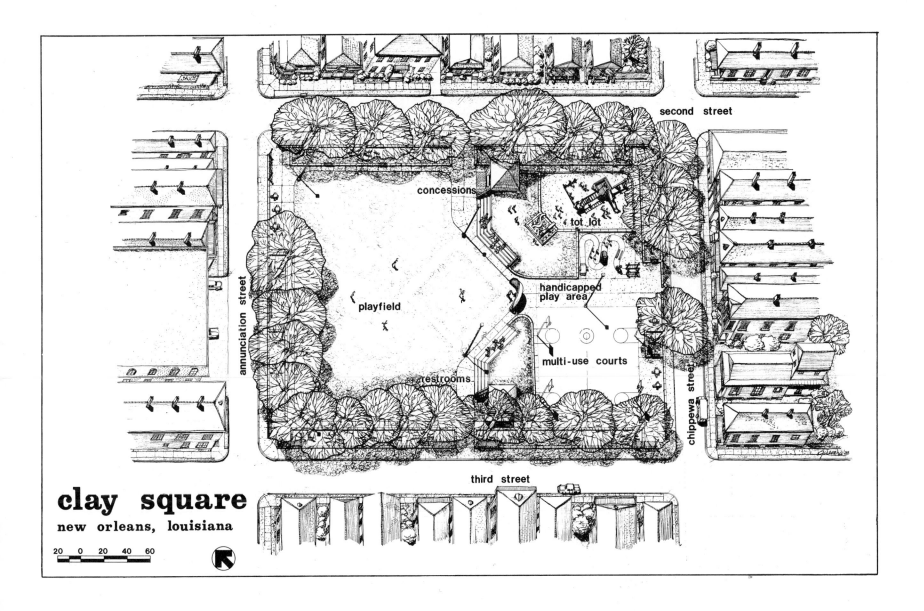

second street

concessions

tot lot

handicapped play area

playfield

multi-use courts

restrooms

annunciation street

chippewa street

third street

clay square

new orleans, louisiana

20 0 20 40 60

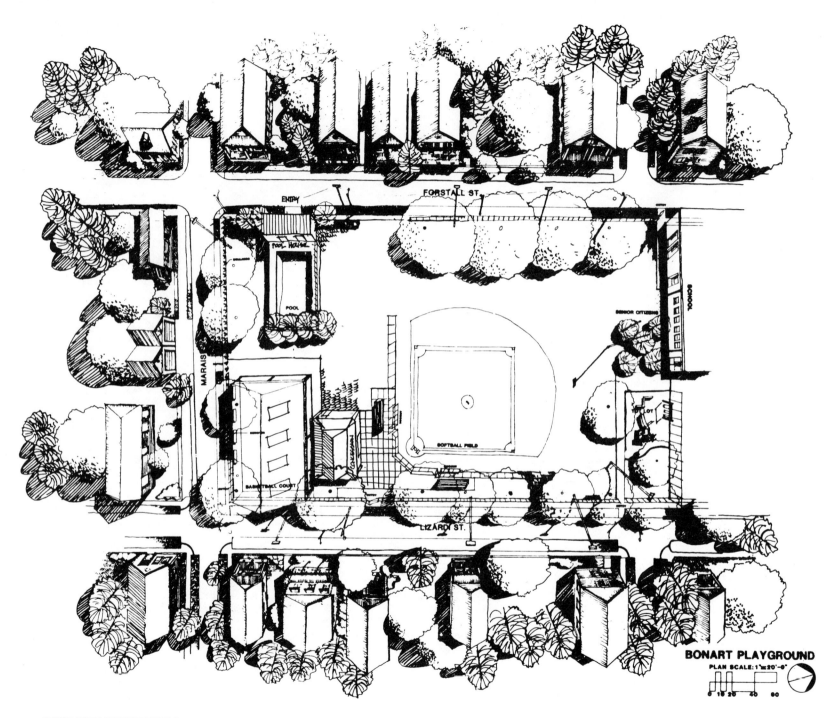

BONART PLAYGROUND

PLAN SCALE: 1"=20'-0"

0 10 20   40   80

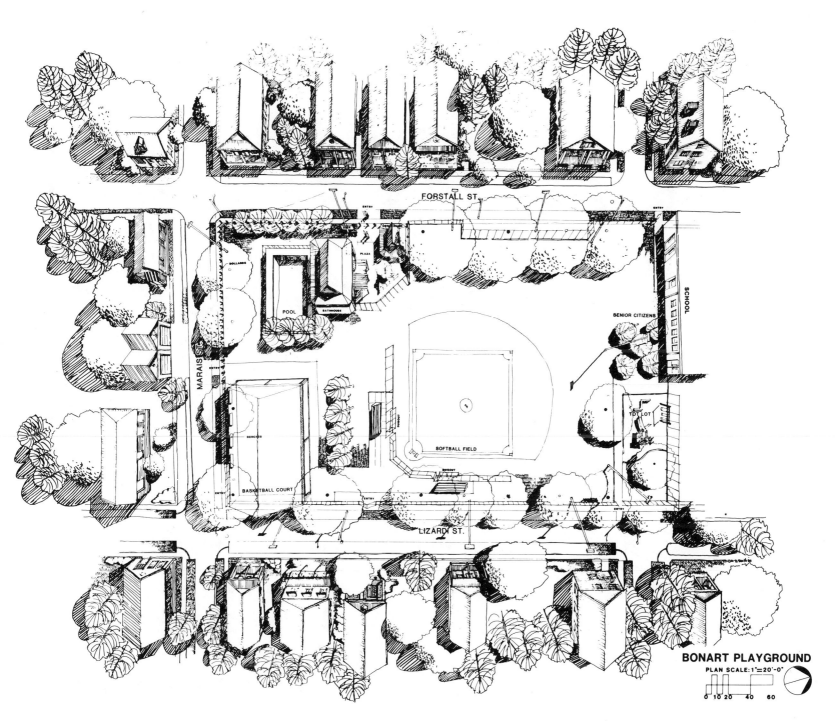

FORSTALL ST.

ENTRY

BENCHES

BOLLARDS

PLAZA

POOL

BATHHOUSE

MARAIS ST.

ENTRY

SCHOOL

SENIOR CITIZENS

BENCHES

DUGOUT

SOFTBALL FIELD

TOT LOT

DUGOUT

ENTRY

BASKETBALL COURT

ENTRY

ENTRY

ENTRY

LIZARDI ST.

BONART PLAYGROUND

PLAN SCALE: 1"=20'-0"

0 10 20   40   60

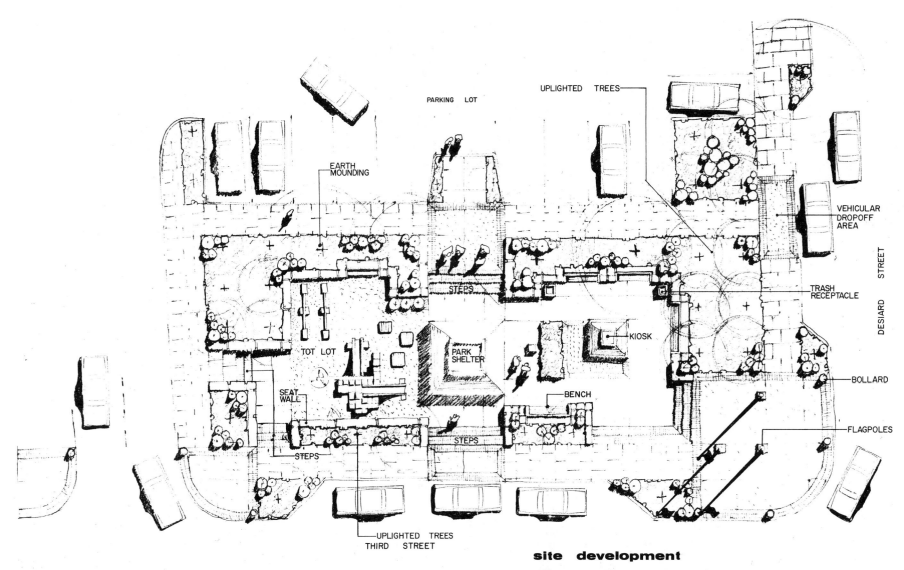

PARKING LOT

UPLIGHTED TREES

EARTH
MOUNDING

VEHICULAR
DROPOFF
AREA

STEPS

TRASH
RECEPTACLE

DESIARD STREET

TOT LOT

KIOSK

PARK
SHELTER

BOLLARD

SEAT
WALL

BENCH

STEPS

FLAGPOLES

STEPS

UPLIGHTED TREES
THIRD STREET

site development

3rd street park

h.h. land architects inc.

cashio·cochran, inc.

landscape architects

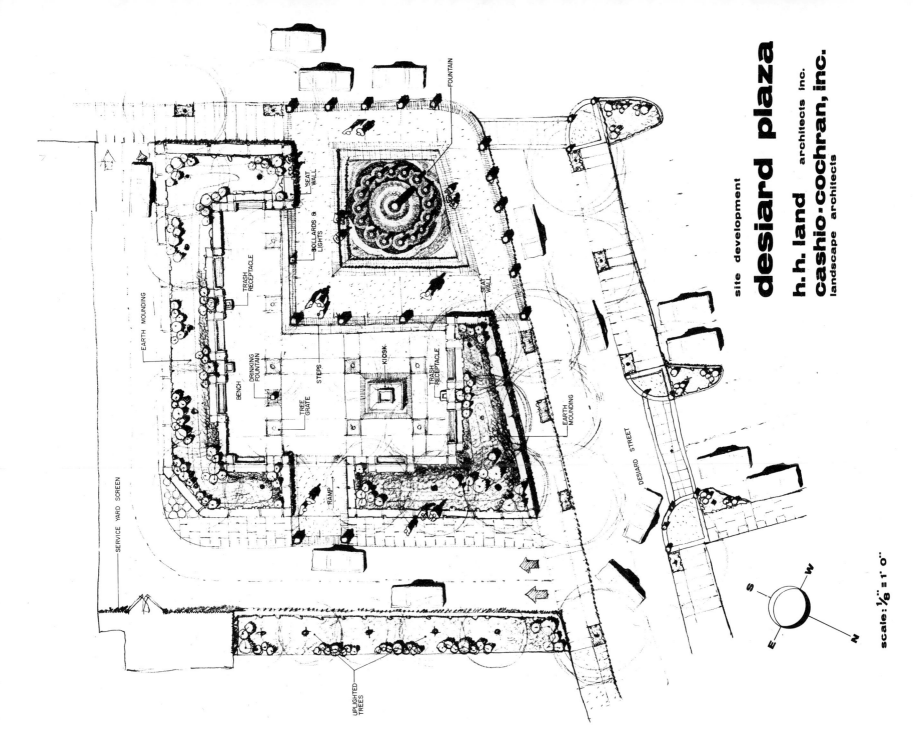

site development

desiard plaza

h. h. land architects inc.

cashio-cochran, inc.
landscape architects

FOUNTAIN

SEAT WALL

BOLLARDS & LIGHTS

TRASH RECEPTACLE

EARTH MOUNDING

DRINKING FOUNTAIN

BENCH

STEPS

TREE GRATE

KIOSK

SEAT WALL

TRASH RECEPTACLE

EARTH MOUNDING

RAMP

DESIARD STREET

SERVICE YARD SCREEN

UPLIGHTED TREES

scale: ⅛" = 1' 0"

Project:	Lowry Park Zoological Garden
Client:	City of Tampa
Location:	Tampa, Florida
Date:	1984–
Presentation:	Blackline with marker
Budget:	$14 million
Status:	Under construction

Lowry Park Zoological Garden is a small (11-acre) zoo in Tampa, Florida. As a result of a comprehensive master plan, the zoo is being expanded to 24 acres to incorporate state-of-the-art exhibits. In this project, as in the Audubon Zoo master plan, complex exhibits—which housed various kinds of animals—were clearly delineated using tilt-ups, which illustrated how walls, rock work, plantings, and the like would be interwoven to form the final design. In this particular project, we worked at two very different scales: the overall 24-acre master plan was done at one inch equals forty feet; the schematic design was drawn at one inch equals twenty feet. The drawing shown is substantially reduced, showing the value of the tilt-up working at various scales. The final scheme was colored and printed as a poster (24 by 36 inches). It has been used as a fund-raising tool as well as a marketing aid.

L. TORRE '81

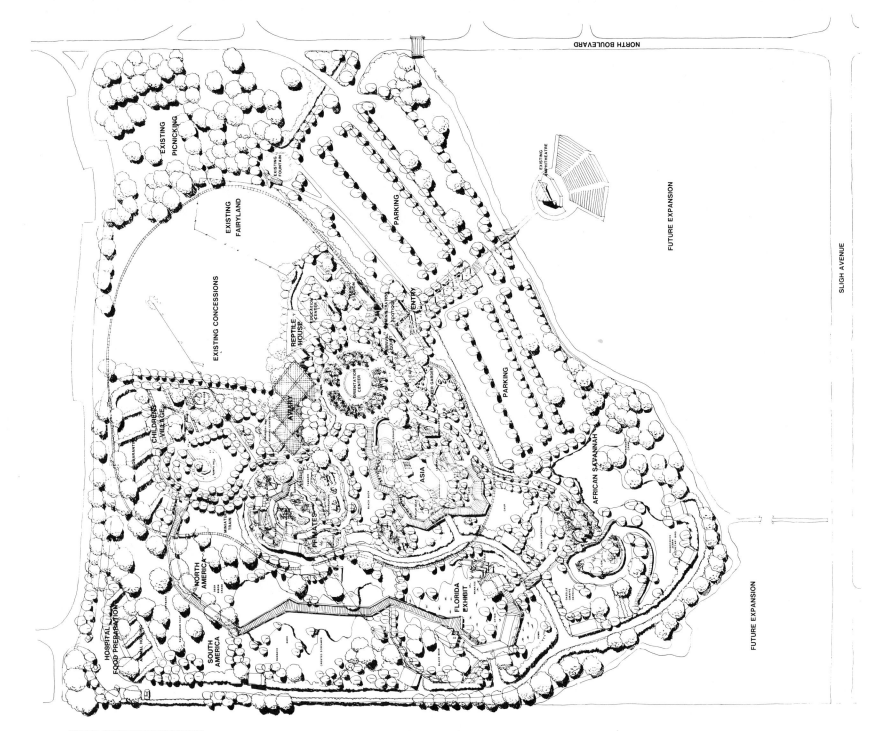

NORTH BOULEVARD

SLIGH AVENUE

FUTURE EXPANSION

FUTURE EXPANSION

EXISTING PICNICKING

EXISTING FAIRYLAND

EXISTING CONCESSIONS

EXISTING FOUNTAIN

EXISTING AMPHITHEATRE

PARKING

PARKING

ENTRY

REPTILE HOUSE

EDUCATION CENTER

ORIENTATION CENTER

ADMINISTRATION

ARRIVAL PLAZA

ZOOTIQUE

CAFE

FLOWER GARDEN

AVIARY

CHILDRENS VILLAGE

QUARANTINE

HOSPITAL

FOOD PREPARATION

ANIMAL HOLDING

NORTH AMERICA

SOUTH AMERICA

PRIMATES

MINIATURE TRAIN

ASIA

FLORIDA EXHIBIT

AFRICAN SAVANNAH

42   SITE PERSPECTIVES

TAMPA'S
LOWRY PARK ZOO

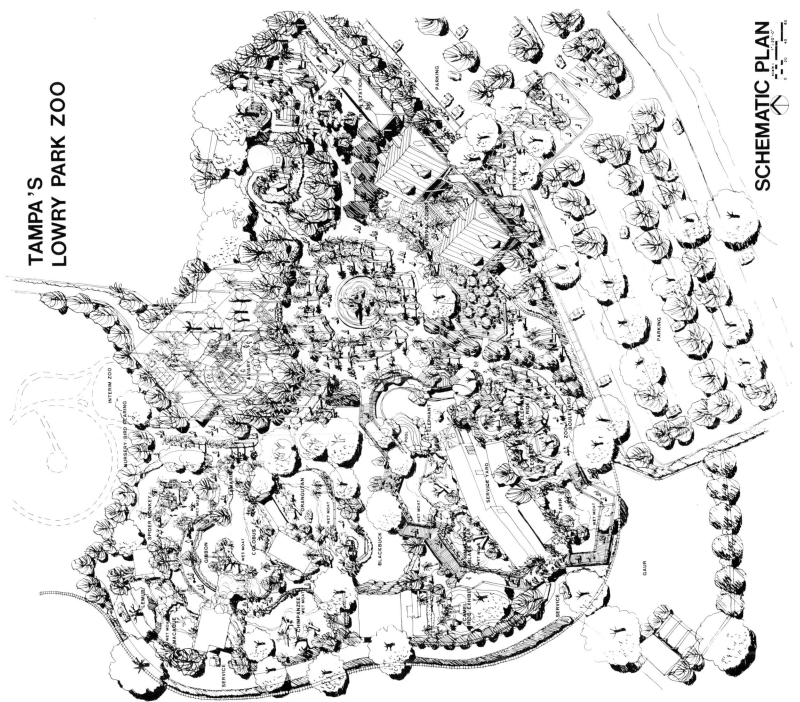

SCHEMATIC PLAN

SECTION 'A' (ENTRY)
SCALE 1"= 10'-0"

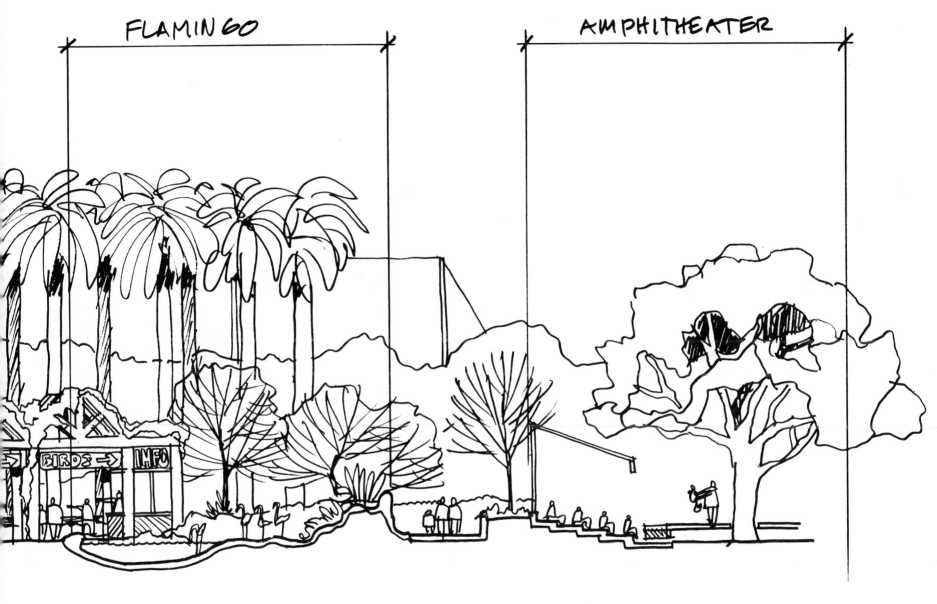

FLAMINGO

AMPHITHEATER

BIRDS → INFO

SECTION 'B' (ARRIVAL COURT)
SCALE 1" = 10'-0"

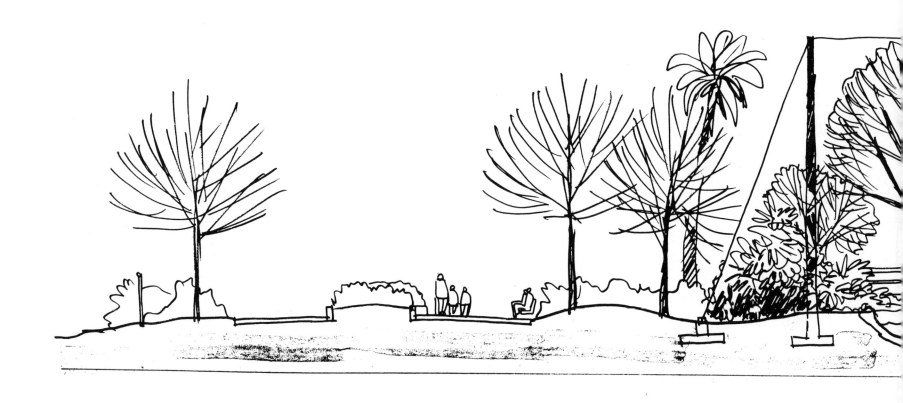

SECTION 'C' (AVIARY)
SCALE 1" = 10'-0"

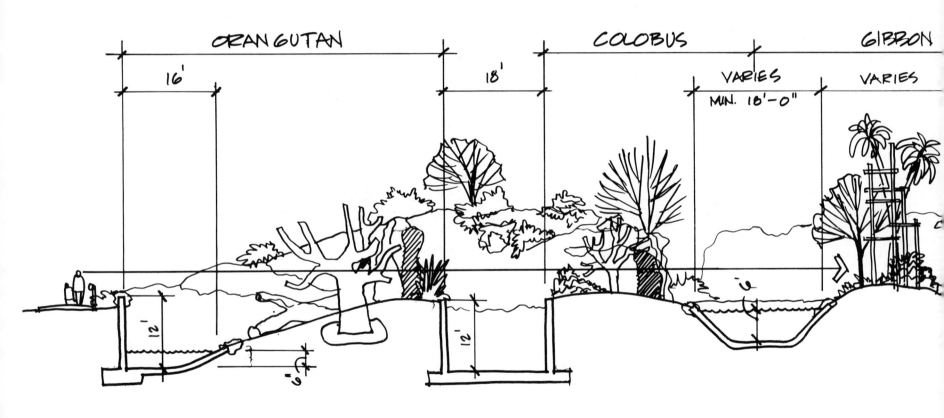

ORANGUTAN   COLOBUS   GIBBON

16'   18'   VARIES   VARIES

MIN. 18'-0"

12'   12'

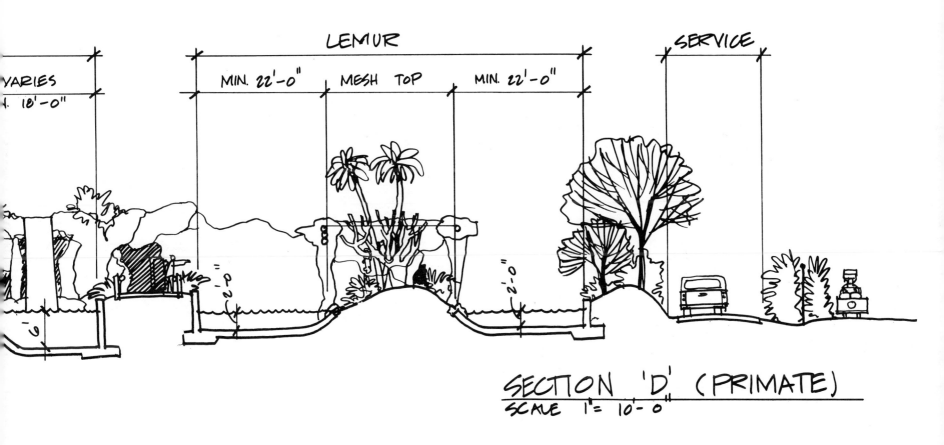

VARIES
N. 18'-0"

LEMUR

MIN. 22'-0" MESH TOP MIN. 22'-0"

SERVICE

2'-0"

SECTION 'D' (PRIMATE)
SCALE 1"= 10'-0"

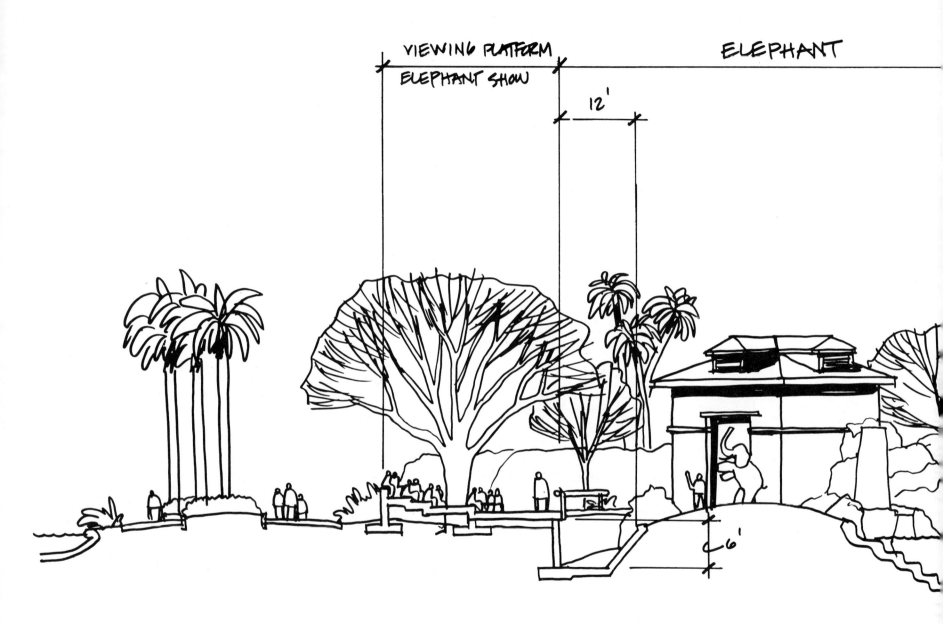

VIEWING PLATFORM ELEPHANT SHOW

ELEPHANT

12'

6'

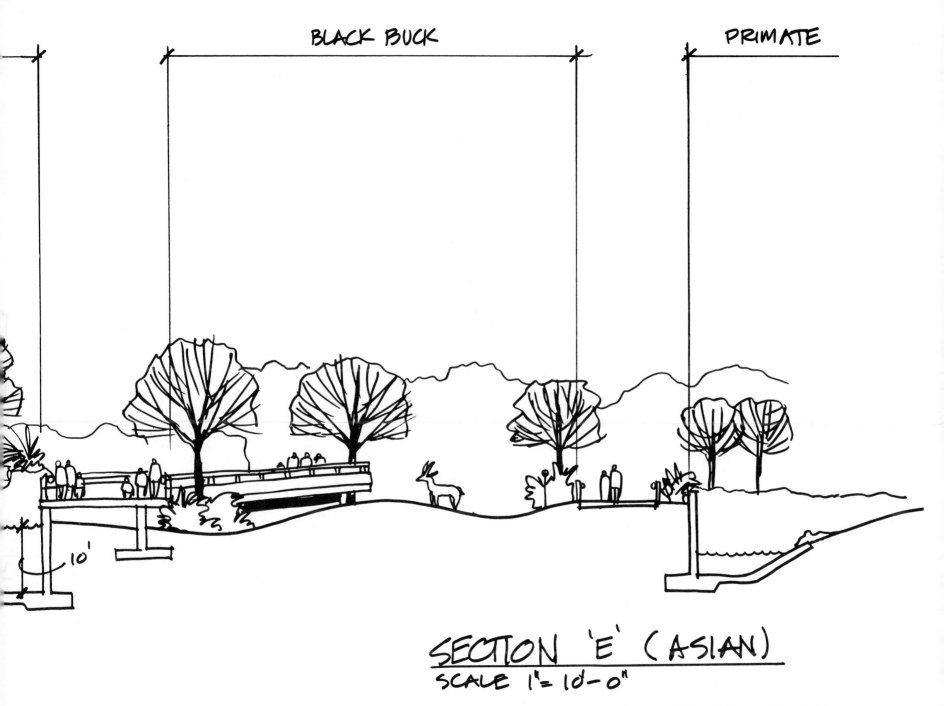

BLACK BUCK

PRIMATE

10'

SECTION 'E' (ASIAN)
SCALE 1"= 10'-0"

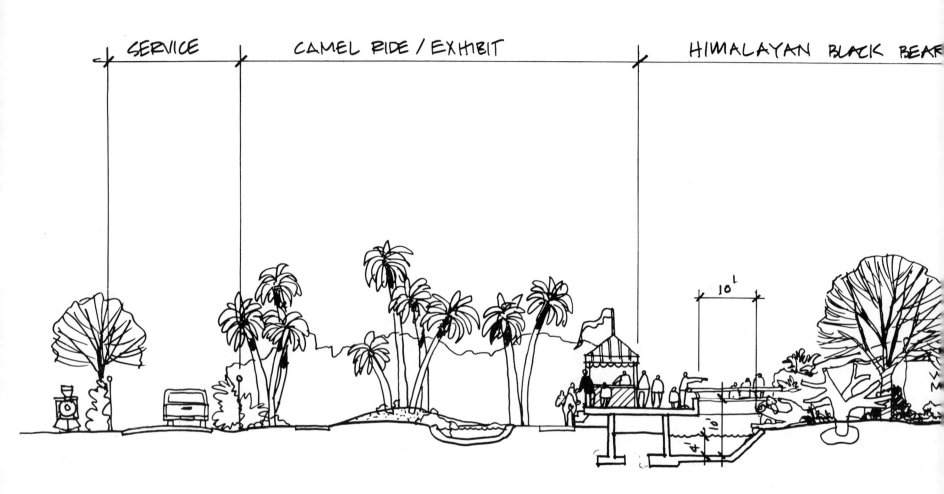

SERVICE   CAMEL RIDE / EXHIBIT   HIMALAYAN BLACK BEAR

10'

10'

4'

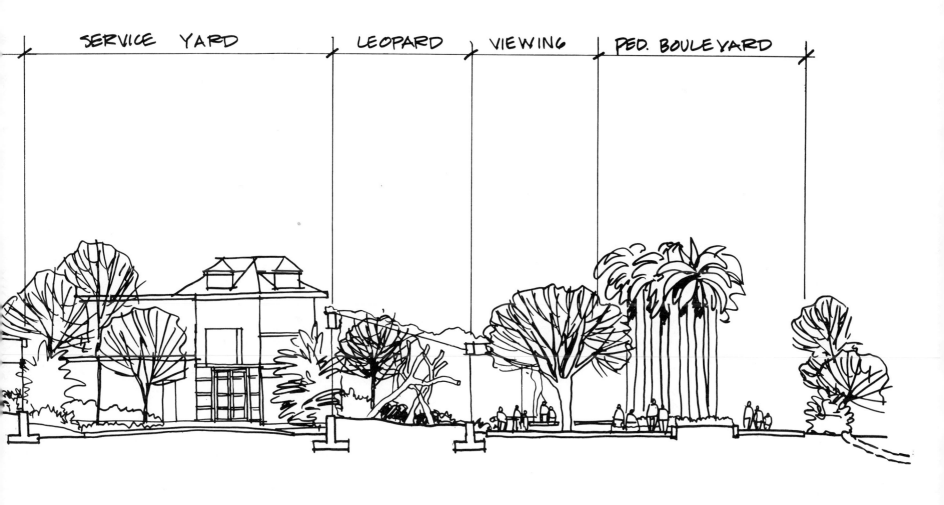

SERVICE YARD | LEOPARD | VIEWING | PED. BOULEVARD

SECTION 'F' (ASIAN)
SCALE 1" = 10'-0"

Project: Busch Gardens
Client: Anheuser-Busch
Location: Tampa, Florida
Date: 1984
Presentation: Pentel, blackline rendered
Budget: $250,000
Status: Complete

Busch Gardens was a very small project (approximately 150 by 100 square feet) designed to perform two major functions: to educate the public about the Bald Eagle (an endangered species and our national symbol), and to illustrate two of this bird's natural habitats—the canyon and the swamp. This project was designed in tilt-up format first, to illustrate general design concepts and to suggest the basic character of the design. It was later transferred to a site plan to produce detailed construction drawings and to work out design details.

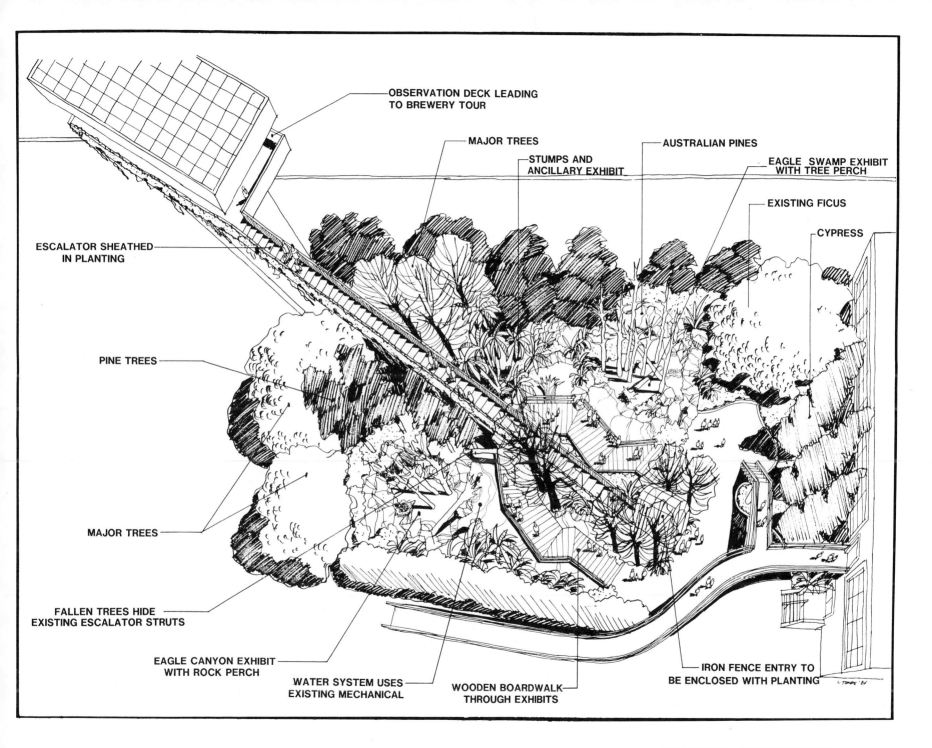

OBSERVATION DECK LEADING
TO BREWERY TOUR

MAJOR TREES

AUSTRALIAN PINES

STUMPS AND
ANCILLARY EXHIBIT

EAGLE SWAMP EXHIBIT
WITH TREE PERCH

EXISTING FICUS

CYPRESS

ESCALATOR SHEATHED
IN PLANTING

PINE TREES

MAJOR TREES

FALLEN TREES HIDE
EXISTING ESCALATOR STRUTS

EAGLE CANYON EXHIBIT
WITH ROCK PERCH

WATER SYSTEM USES
EXISTING MECHANICAL

WOODEN BOARDWALK
THROUGH EXHIBITS

IRON FENCE ENTRY TO
BE ENCLOSED WITH PLANTING

Project:	Louisiana Nature Center
Client:	Louisiana Nature Center
Location:	New Orleans, Louisiana
Date:	1984
Presentation:	Rendered blackline
Budget:	$600,000
Status:	Under construction
Associated Professionals:	E. Eean McNaughton, Architect

On the basis of previous successful projects such as the Audubon Zoo in New Orleans, and the Mississippi Nature Center in Pascagoula, Design Consortium was selected to renovate and expand the Louisiana Nature Center facility. The goal was to create a building footprint that would satisfy program requirements for exhibits, seminars, educational functions, and the like, and to accommodate outdoor activities, exhibits, and vistas into the center's swamp setting. The tilt-up drawing—completed in about 3 hours—illustrated the proposed additions to the center and suggested opportunities for program development. In so doing, the facility was recognized as an important amenity to the community, and public support and sponsorship for the project was thus generated.

LOUISIANA NATURE CENTER EXPANSION

ACCESS

PARKING

PARKING

WILDLIFE GARDEN

FRESH WATER POND

EXISTING ENTRY

EXISTING NATURE CENTER

GREEN MARSH

ACTIVE SOLAR

GREENHOUSE

PINES

PAVILION

NATIVE WILDFLOWERS

FOOD CONCESSION

CYPRESS SWAMP

EDUCATION COMPLEX RESOURCE CENTER

MASSIVE SOLAR STUDY AREA

OUTDOOR STUDY SUPPORT LAB

CYPRESS SWAMP

EXHIBIT PREPARATION

CLAM SHELL COURT

PROGRAM DEVELOPMENT

ADMINISTRATION

OBSERVATION TOWER

PLANETARIUM & MULTI-MEDIA

NATURAL PLANTS AND EXHIBITS

INDIAN MIDDEN

LOGJAM

TRAILS

BAYOU ENVIRONMENT

OPEN STORAGE

FIELDS OF SENECIO

MAGNOLIAS AND OAKS ON RIDGES

TRAIL BRIDGE

TRAILS

BLACK WILLOWS

PROJECTS: RECREATION   67

Project:	Louis Armstrong Park Development Proposal
Client:	City of New Orleans
Location:	New Orleans
Date:	1982
Presentation:	Blackline with color
Budget:	$7 million
Status:	Complete
Associated Professionals:	Robin Riley, Architect

Design Consortium played two roles in designing the Louis Armstrong Park, serving first as urban designer/landscape architect for the initial design of the park in the 1970s; and subsequently as a developer for a proposed redevelopment of the complex. In the early phases of the project, drawings similar to the one shown were used to illustrate the basic infrastructure of the park, which is now complete. In 1982, we were asked to submit a proposal for the overall development of the park. We established long-range design goals geared toward creating a self-sufficient and diverse cultural park for New Orleans. The tilt-up provided a flexible working drawing that illustrated the overall cultural goal and the underlying theme of the development, without committing to exact details. It gave us an opportunity to depict an overall image for the proposed development.

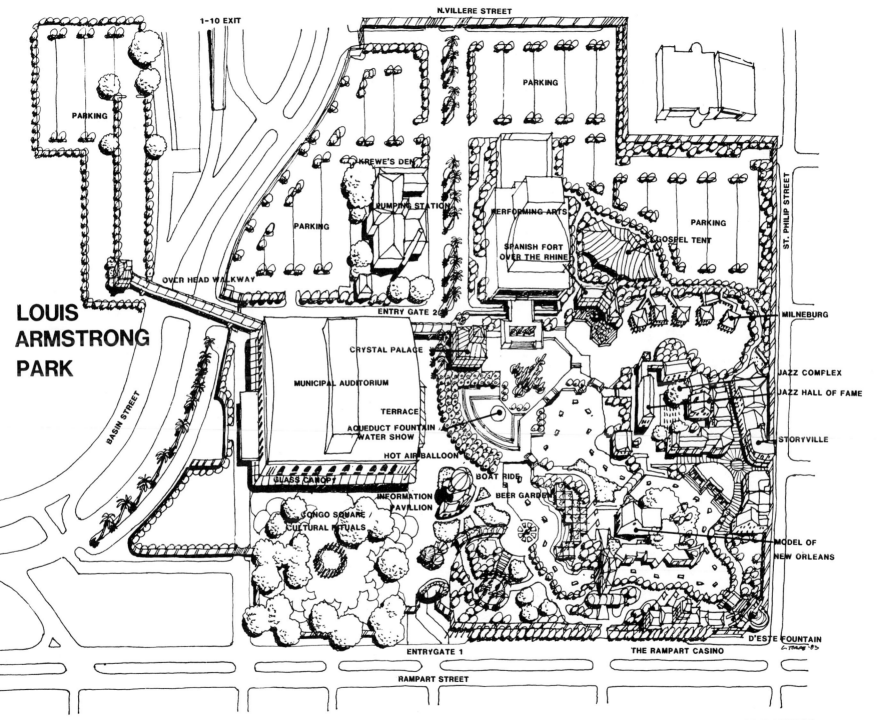

LOUIS
ARMSTRONG
PARK

N. VILLERE STREET

I-10 EXIT

PARKING

PARKING

PARKING

KREWE'S DEN

PUMPING STATION

PARKING

PERFORMING ARTS

SPANISH FORT
OVER THE RHINE

GOSPEL TENT

ST. PHILIP STREET

OVER HEAD WALKWAY

ENTRY GATE 2

MILNEBURG

BASIN STREET

CRYSTAL PALACE

MUNICIPAL AUDITORIUM

TERRACE

AQUEDUCT FOUNTAIN
WATER SHOW

HOT AIR BALLOON

GLASS CANOPY

BOAT RIDE
&
BEER GARDEN

INFORMATION
PAVILLION

CONGO SQUARE
CULTURAL RITUALS

JAZZ COMPLEX

JAZZ HALL OF FAME

STORYVILLE

MODEL OF
NEW ORLEANS

D'ESTE FOUNTAIN

ENTRY GATE 1

THE RAMPART CASINO

RAMPART STREET

WATERFRONTS

Project: Biloxi Master Plan
Client: City of Biloxi
Location: Biloxi, Mississippi
Date   1984–
Presentation: Blackline with marker
Budget: $70 million
Status: In progress
Associated Professionals: NY Associates, Architects, New Orleans, LA

The master plan for the Biloxi, Mississippi waterfront provided for the development of approximately five linear miles of beachfront on the Gulf of Mexico, with a critical activity center at its easterly point, Point Cadet. The use of the plan was ancillary to the tilt-up design in this project. The tilt-up drawings preceded the plan in this case, and the plan was used to define and implement the suggested design solutions with relative accuracy. The city has subsequently used these drawings in civic information presentations and publications.

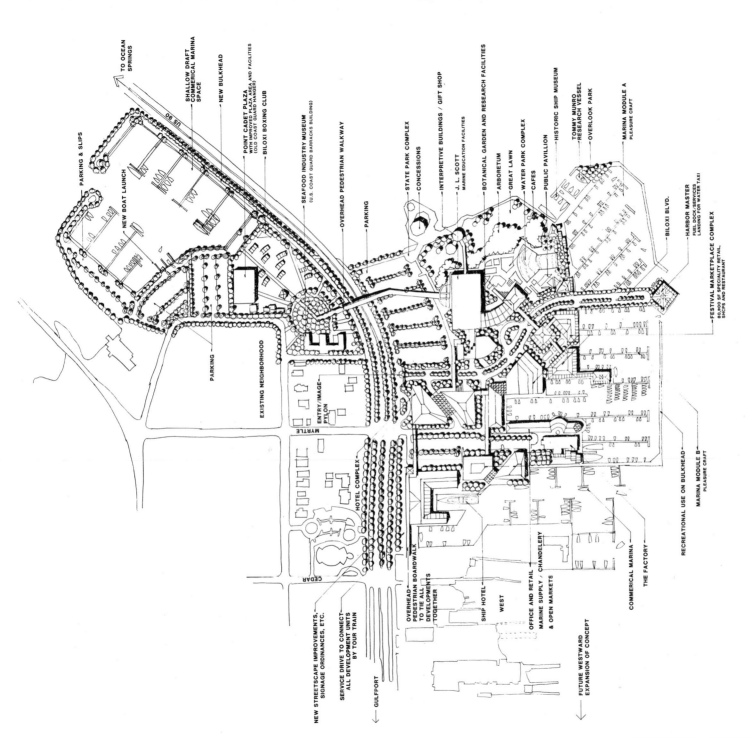

PARKING & SLIPS

TO OCEAN SPRINGS

US 90

NEW BOAT LAUNCH

SHALLOW DRAFT COMMERICAL MARINA SPACE

NEW BULKHEAD

POINT CADET PLAZA
WITH IMPROVED PLAZA AREA AND FACILITIES
(OLD COAST GUARD HANGER)

BILOXI BOXING CLUB

SEAFOOD INDUSTRY MUSEUM
(U.S. COAST GUARD BARRACKS BUILDING)

OVERHEAD PEDESTRIAN WALKWAY

PARKING

STATE PARK COMPLEX

CONCESSIONS

INTERPRETIVE BUILDINGS / GIFT SHOP

J. L. SCOTT
MARINE EDUCATION FACILITIES

BOTANICAL GARDEN AND RESEARCH FACILITIES

ARBORETUM

GREAT LAWN

WATER PARK COMPLEX

CAFES

PUBLIC PAVILLION

HISTORIC SHIP MUSEUM

TOMMY MUNRO
RESEARCH VESSEL

OVERLOOK PARK

MARINA MODULE A
PLEASURE CRAFT

BILOXI BLVD.

HARBOR MASTER
FUEL DOCK/SERVICES
LANDING FOR WATER TAXI

FESTIVAL MARKETPLACE COMPLEX
80,000 SF SPECIALITY RETAIL,
SHOPS AND RESTAURANT

RECREATIONAL USE ON BULKHEAD

MARINA MODULE B
PLEASURE CRAFT

COMMERICAL MARINA

THE FACTORY

FUTURE WESTWARD
EXPANSION OF CONCEPT

OFFICE AND RETAIL

MARINE SUPPLY / CHANDELERY
& OPEN MARKETS

WEST

SHIP HOTEL

OVERHEAD
PEDESTRIAN BOARDWALK
TO TIE ALL
DEVELOPMENTS
TOGETHER

SERVICE DRIVE TO CONNECT
ALL DEVELOPMENT UNITS
BY TOUR TRAIN

NEW STREETSCAPE IMPROVEMENTS,
SIGNAGE ORDINANCES, ETC.

GULFPORT

CEDAR

MYRTLE

HOTEL COMPLEX

ENTRY/IMAGE
PYLON

EXISTING NEIGHBORHOOD

PARKING

POINT CADET STUDY AREA
BILOXI WATERFRONT MASTER PLAN
BILOXI, MISSISSIPPI

NORTH

Project: Pascagoula Waterfront
Client: City of Pascagoula
Location: Pascagoula, Mississippi
Date: 1982–84
Presentation: Blackline; study report
Budget: $20 million
Status: Phase One complete

The Pascagoula waterfront was planned from a diverse array of perspective sketches, tilt-ups, and plan views. A series of sketches was used to analyze design options and to adapt and modify the final plan.

Working through tilt-ups of the Pascagoula Nature Center, we were able to define the interrelationships of architecture, site development, natural elements, and environmental systems indigenous to the area. The tilt-up provided the basis for an architectural image for the development and led to the construction of a building model.

A unique feature is the *Scranton*—a 76-foot-long steel shrimp trawler. It is permanently moored and now houses aquariums, an amphitheater, learning exhibits, and renovated living quarters for the crew. Cut-away drawings were used in the original presentation and were effective in enabling the client to understand clearly what the scope of the project could be.

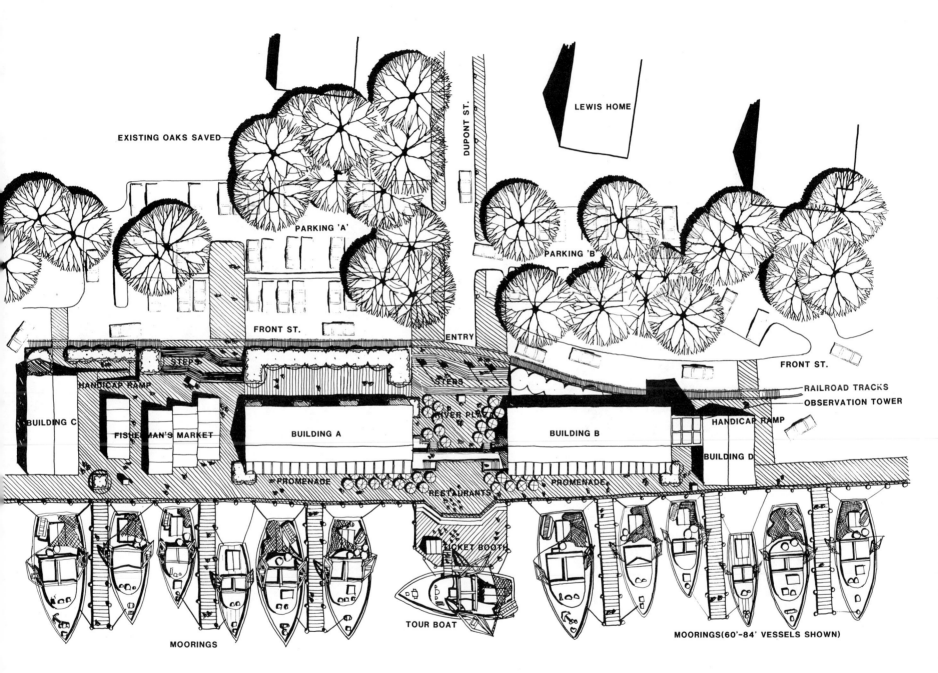

EXISTING OAKS SAVED

DUPONT ST.

LEWIS HOME

PARKING 'A'

PARKING 'B'

FRONT ST.

ENTRY

FRONT ST.

STEPS

STEPS

RAILROAD TRACKS

OBSERVATION TOWER

HANDICAP RAMP

BUILDING C

FISHERMAN'S MARKET

BUILDING A

RIVER PLA

BUILDING B

HANDICAP RAMP

BUILDING D

PROMENADE

RESTAURANTS

PROMENADE

TICKET BOOTH

MOORINGS

TOUR BOAT

MOORINGS(60'-84' VESSELS SHOWN)

EAST PASCAGOULA RIVER

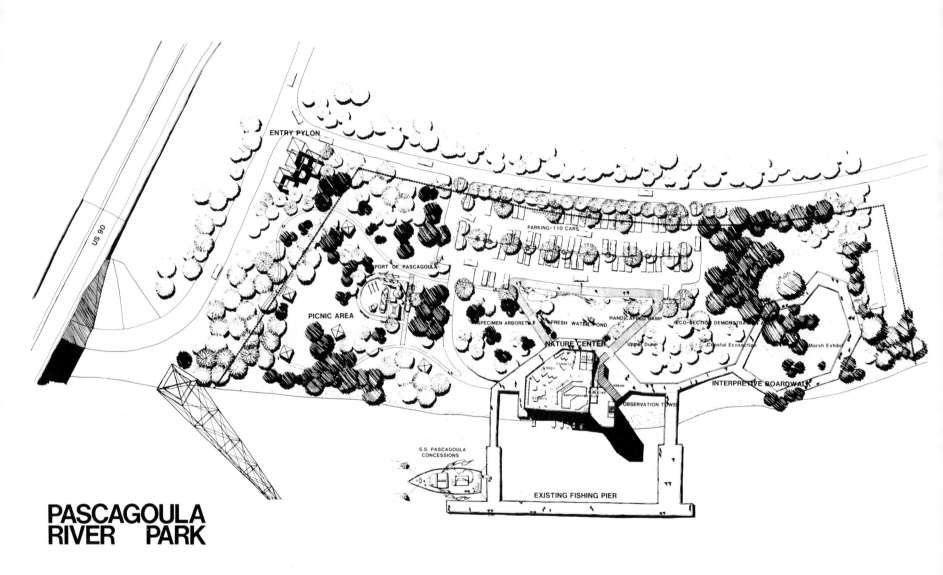

ENTRY PYLON

PARKING-110 CARS

PORT OF PASCAGOULA

PICNIC AREA

SPECIMEN ARBORETUM   FRESH WATER POND   HANDICAPPED RAMP   ECO-SECTION DEMONSTRATION

NATURE CENTER   Upper Dune   Coastal Ecosection   Marsh Exhibit

EXHIBITS   REST ROOMS
EXHIBITS
EXHIBITS   AMPHITHEATER   ARBOR   OBSERVATION TOWER

INTERPRETIVE BOARDWALK

S.S. PASCAGOULA
CONCESSIONS

EXISTING FISHING PIER

US 90

PASCAGOULA
RIVER PARK

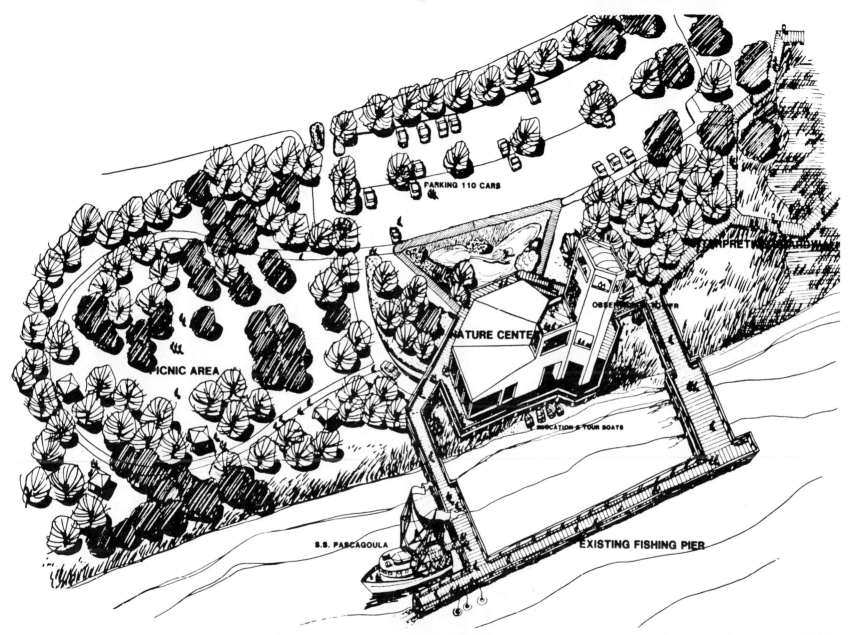

PARKING 110 CARS

INTERPRETIVE BOARDWALK

OBSERVATION TOWER

NATURE CENTER

PICNIC AREA

EDUCATION & TOUR BOATS

S.S. PASCAGOULA

EXISTING FISHING PIER

MISSISSIPPI NATURE CENTER
PASCAGOULA RIVER PARK

L. TORRE '82

PORT OF PASCAGOULA TOT LOT

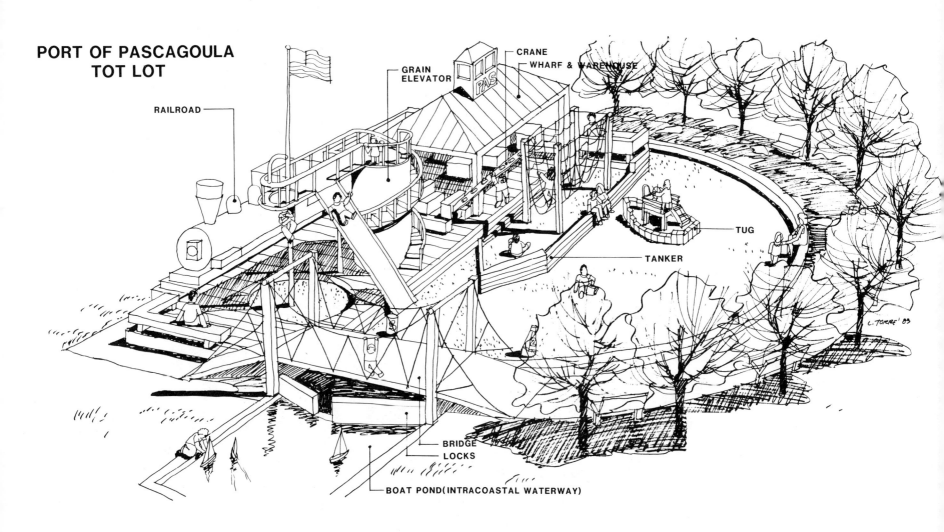

RAILROAD

GRAIN ELEVATOR

CRANE
WHARF & WAREHOUSE

TUG

TANKER

BRIDGE
LOCKS

BOAT POND(INTRACOASTAL WATERWAY)

L. TORRE '83

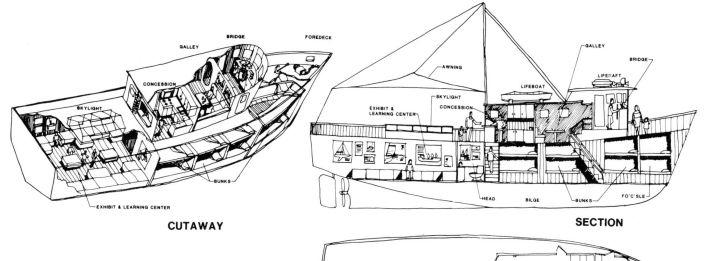

CUTAWAY

SECTION

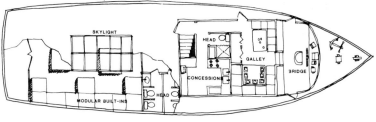

PLAN

SCRANTON MUSEUM

ELEVATION

Project: Jefferson Parish Recreation Master Plan
Client: Jefferson Parish
Location: Jefferson Parish, Louisiana
Date: 1982
Presentation: Pentel, blackline prints, rendered
Budget: $40 million
Status: In progress

The Jefferson Parish Recreation Master Plan was an index to the recreation potential and opportunities for the entire 1200-square-mile parish area. A survey of the area was conducted first by helicopter and then at ground level. The initial design was actually created from aerial views of the site and then reassessed and refined after a closer examination from the ground. This project relied heavily on the tilt-up drawings because they provided specific points of reference, which facilitated the presentation of general concepts for the development of a very large geographic area. In the final master plan publication, tilt-ups were shown with aerial photographs of existing facilities to illustrate the proposed improvements. Tilt-ups were also used to show how existing parks could be linked with proposed developments to create a comprehensive, parishwide recreation plan.

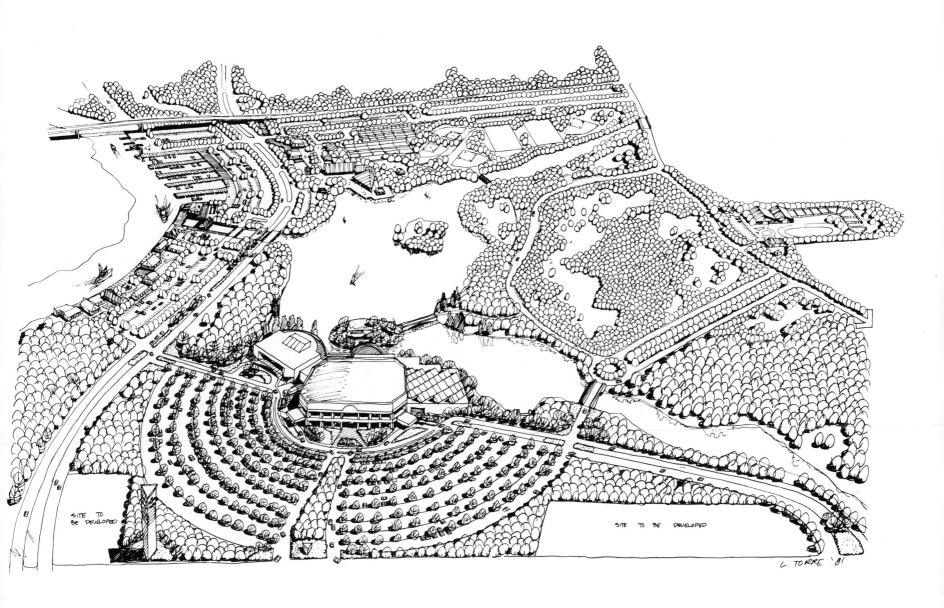

SITE TO
BE DEVELOPED

SITE TO BE DEVELOPED

L. TORRE '81

L. TORRE '81

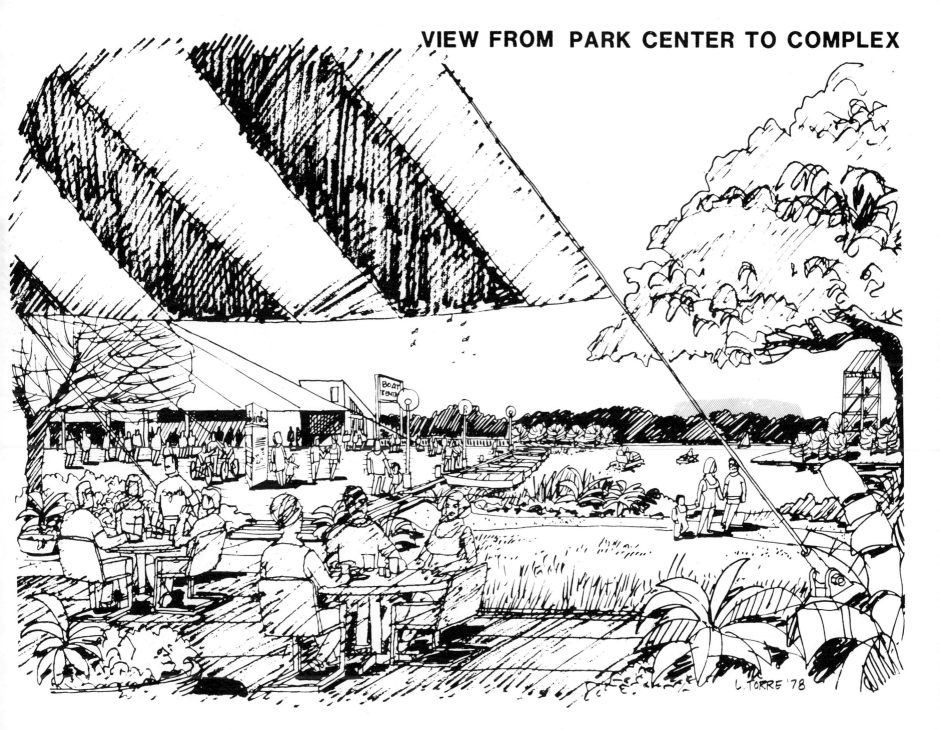

L. TORRE '78

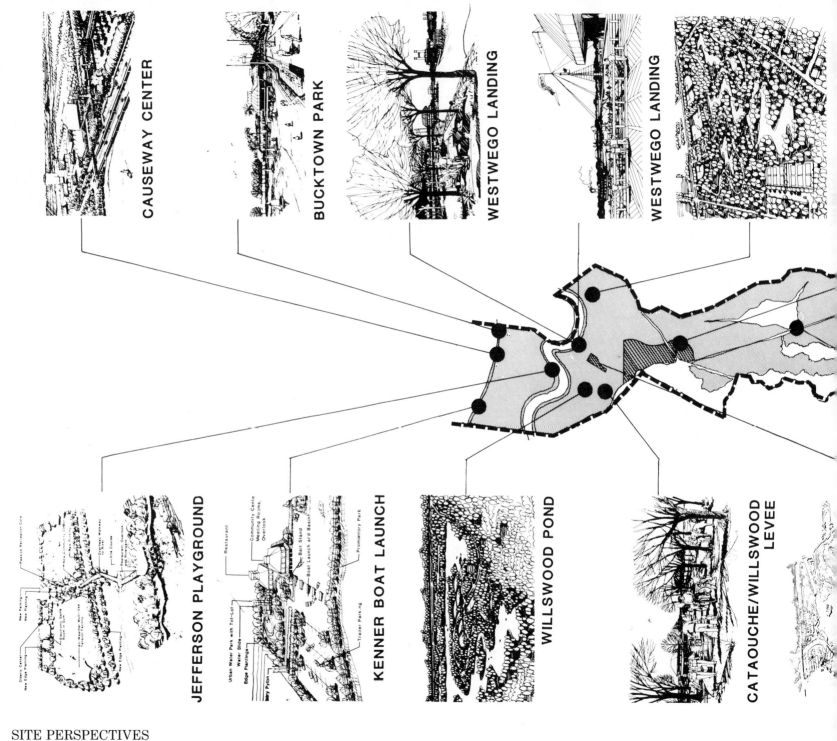

CAUSEWAY CENTER

BUCKTOWN PARK

WESTWEGO LANDING

WESTWEGO LANDING

JEFFERSON PLAYGROUND

KENNER BOAT LAUNCH

WILLSWOOD POND

CATAOUCHE/WILLSWOOD LEVEE

JEAN LAFITTE
NATIONAL PARK

FORT LIVINGSTON

BAYOU SEGNETTE
STATE PARK

HUGHES MARINA

JEFFERSON PARISH RECREATION MASTER PLAN

The proposed master plan attempts to connect and overlap the different zones of the Parish with proposed recreational use throughout the Parish. The first zone is the Lake Pontchartrain Linear Park which would include the Bucktown Park, Causeway Center, Bonnabel Boat Launch, and Kenner Boat Launch developments. Next would be the levee systems on both banks of the Mississippi River, including the Jefferson Playground/ River Overlook, and the Westwego Landing developments. The swamp/ marshland condition which comprises the majority of the Parish could include such projects as the Willswood Pond area, the Cataouche/ Willswood Levee areas, and use of the Bayou Segnette State Park and Jean Lafitte National Park. The last zone and the southernmost point of the Parish would be the barrier islands, where a development utilizing Fort Livingston would round out a Parish-wide recreational system. This system, for the first time, will be instrumental in creating a united Jefferson Parish.

Project: St. Bernard State Park
Client: St. Bernard Parish
Location: St. Bernard Parish, Louisiana
Date: 1973
Presentation: Pentel, blackline prints, rendered
Budget: $4 million
Status: Complete

St. Bernard State Park is a 200-acre park that offers numerous recreation facilities, including campgrounds, and the unique opportunity to develop a physical connection with the Mississippi River. A major docking station was designed and delineated with an aerial tilt-up, which indicated its location on the river and the opportunities for linkages between downtown areas and the state park.

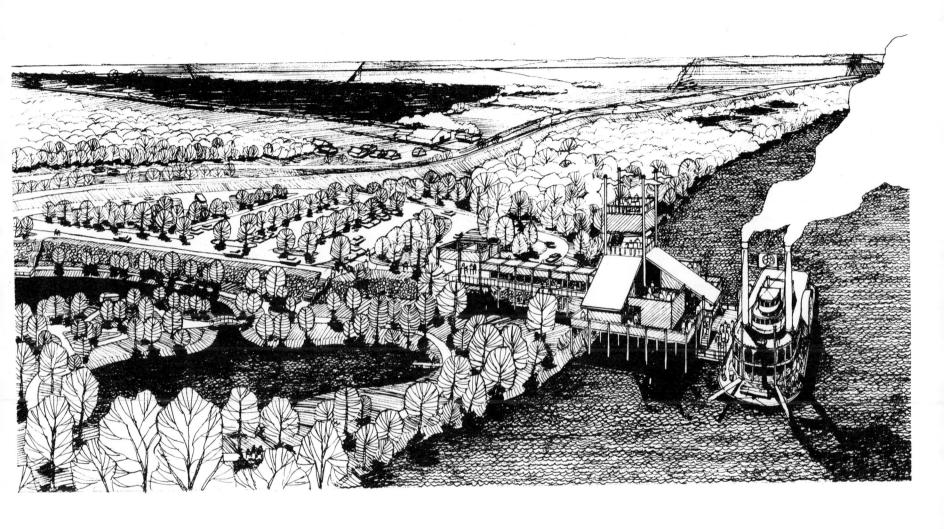

Project: Southbank Riverwalk
Client: City of Jacksonville
Location: Jacksonville, Florida
Date: 1982–84
Presentation: Promotional color brochure
Budget: $6 million
Status: Under construction
Associated Professionals: Perkins and Partners, Architects, New Orleans

The Southbank Riverwalk project consists of 1.5 miles of waterfront on the St. John's River. Recent development has created a tremendous amount of new office space but no particular focal points for recreation or marine activities and no consideration of, or accommodations for, the public use of the waterfront. The tilt-up proved to be an effective tool for delineating development potentials for the City Council, concerned businesses, and the public. The tilt-up was critical in this case, because it showed clearly the project in its entirety and allowed each client/user to understand the benefits of the project in relation to themselves and the surrounding areas. Issues such as the opening of the water's edge to more tourism, accommodating river traffic, and connecting and improving access routes between the north and south sides of the river, were addressed and resolved using the tilt-up drawings.

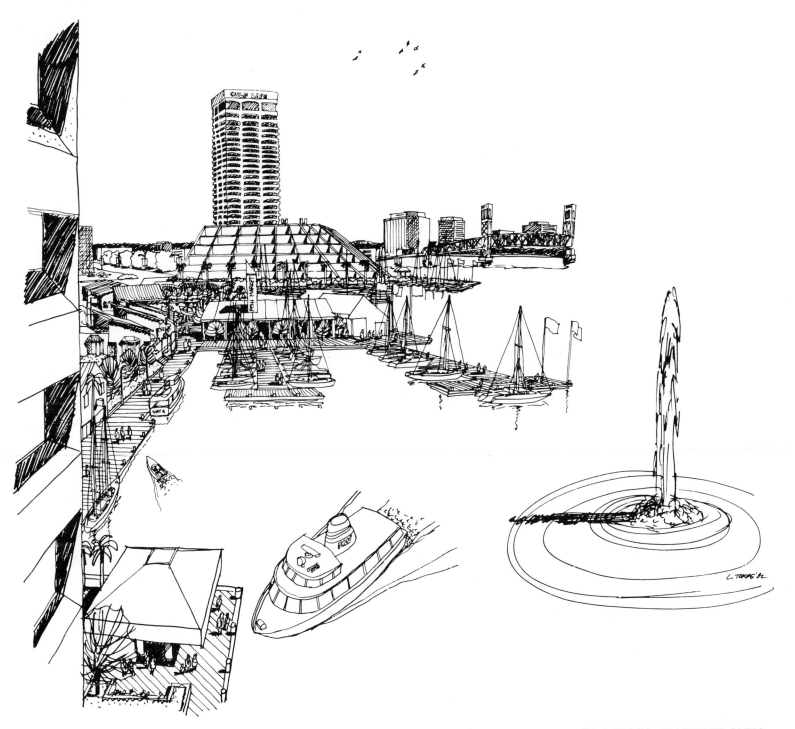

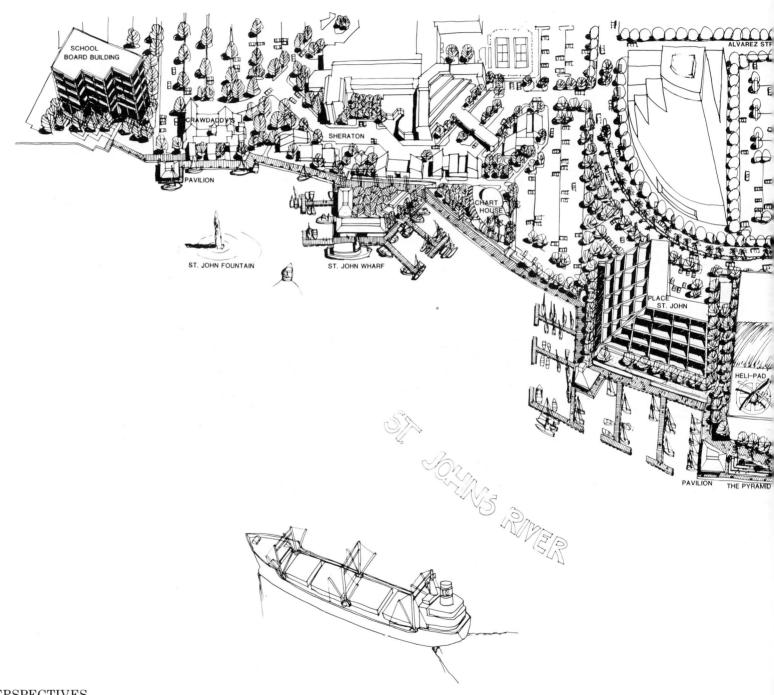

SCHOOL
BOARD BUILDING

ALVAREZ ST

CRAWDADDY'S

SHERATON

PAVILION

CHART
HOUSE

ST. JOHN FOUNTAIN

ST. JOHN WHARF

PLACE
ST. JOHN

HELI-PAD

ST. JOHNS RIVER

PAVILION   THE PYRAMID

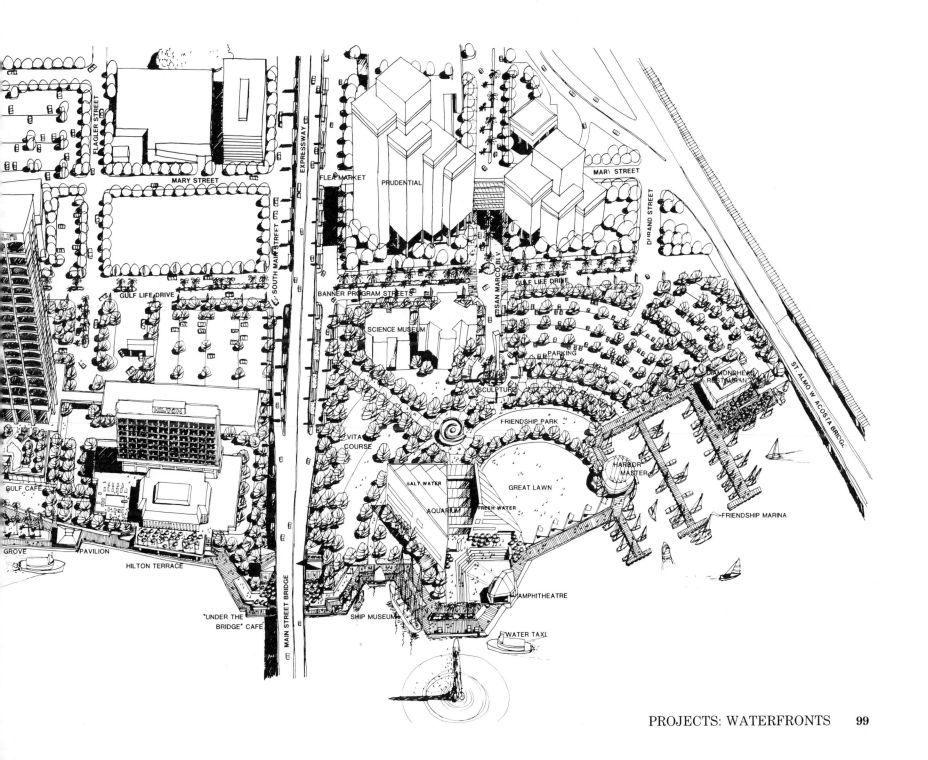

FLAGLER STREET

MARY STREET

SOUTH MAIN STREET

EXPRESSWAY

FLEA MARKET

PRUDENTIAL

MARY STREET

D'URAND STREET

GULF LIFE DRIVE

BANNER PROGRAM STREETS

SAN MARCO BLV.

GULF LIFE DRIVE

PARKING

SCIENCE MUSEUM

ST. ALMO W ACOSTA BRIDGE

DIAMONDHEAD RESTAURANT

SCULPTURE

HILTON

VITA COURSE

FRIENDSHIP PARK

HARBOR MASTER

GULF CAFE

SALT WATER

GREAT LAWN

FRESH WATER

AQUARIUM

FRIENDSHIP MARINA

GROVE

PAVILION

HILTON TERRACE

AMPHITHEATRE

"UNDER THE BRIDGE" CAFE

MAIN STREET BRIDGE

SHIP MUSEUM

WATER TAXI

Project:	Audubon Landing
Client:	Audubon Zoological Garden
Location:	New Orleans, Louisiana
Date:	1983
Presentation:	Promotional color brochure
Budget:	$7 million
Status:	Under construction

The Audubon Landing project had to be "sold" to the public. The tilt-up drawings offered a comprehensive visual package—illustrating all of the components of the project—that the public could understand and accept. Three eye-level sketches, which delineated the three component spaces of the overall design, were also used in the presentation, to provide realistic glimpses of the final project. These drawings were incorporated into a four-color promotional brochure which has been successful in "selling" the project to the community.

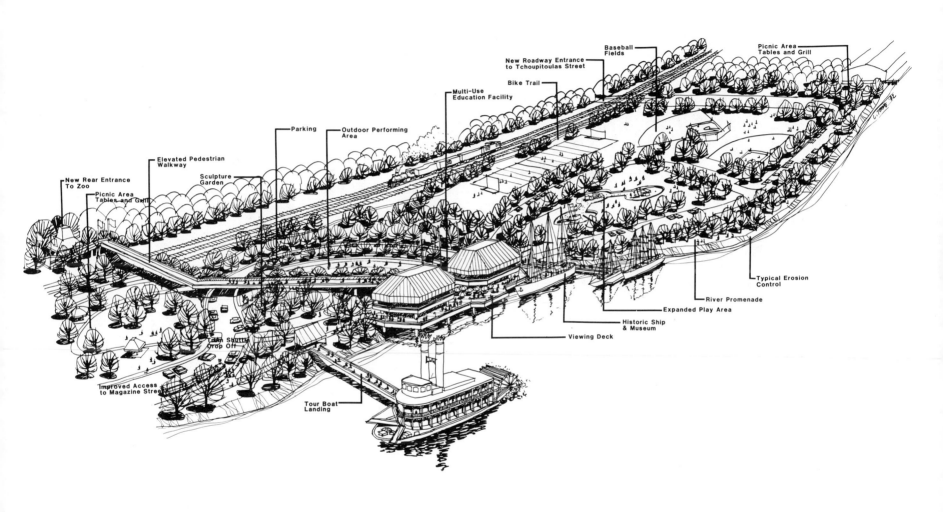

New Rear Entrance
To Zoo

Picnic Area
Tables and Grill

Elevated Pedestrian
Walkway

Sculpture
Garden

Parking

Outdoor Performing
Area

Multi-Use
Education Facility

Bike Trail

New Roadway Entrance
to Tchoupitoulas Street

Baseball
Fields

Picnic Area
Tables and Grill

Typical Erosion
Control

River Promenade

Expanded Play Area

Historic Ship
& Museum

Viewing Deck

Improved Access
to Magazine Street

Tour Boat
Landing

PROJECTS: WATERFRONTS   101

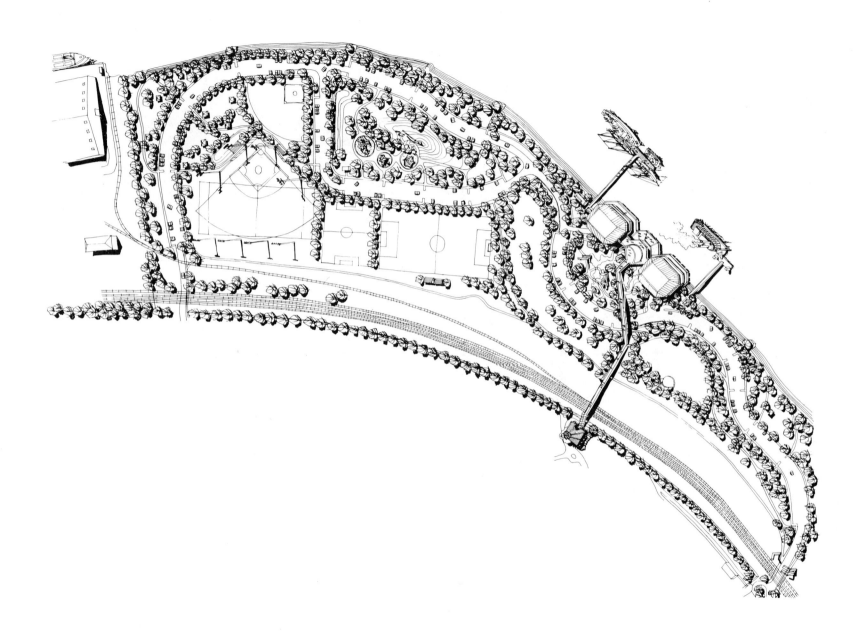

Project: Vieux Carre Riverfront Improvements
Client: City of New Orleans
Location: New Orleans, Louisiana
Date: 1974–76
Presentation: Colored blackline
Budget: $10 million
Status: Complete

The Vieux Carre Riverfront project, winner of the 1981 ASLA Honor
Award, was developed through a series of projects that began with connecting
Jackson Square to the riverfront. The riverfront was subsequently linked with
renovated buildings, farmers' markets, and open spaces in the French Market
area of the Vieux Carre. The tilt-up was used to illustrate the evolution of the
project. It defined the linkages between the various components of the
riverfront—the Washington Artillery Park, the French Market buildings, the
plazas, the farmers' market, and the Old Mint. Tilt-ups were later used to
analyze how a more complex array of land uses—that is, additional and multi-
use areas—could be incorporated into the open plaza spaces, to provide a
broader base for activities and to increase patronage of the riverfront.

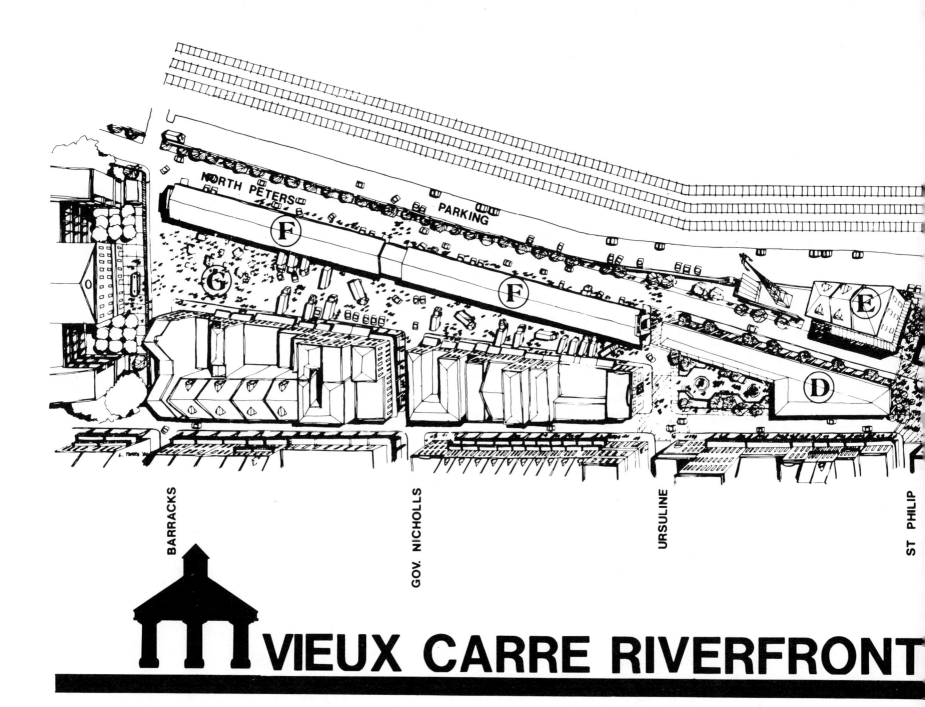

PARKING

NORTH PETERS

F

G

F

E

D

BARRACKS

GOV. NICHOLLS

URSULINE

ST PHILIP

VIEUX CARRE RIVERFRONT

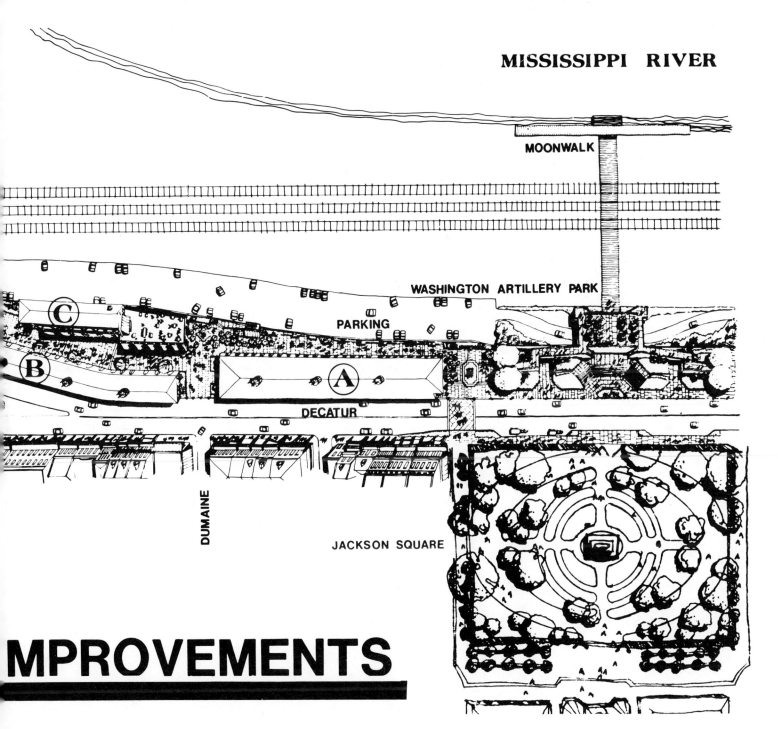

MISSISSIPPI RIVER

MOONWALK

WASHINGTON ARTILLERY PARK

PARKING

C

B

A

DECATUR

DUMAINE

JACKSON SQUARE

MPROVEMENTS

Project: Port West Marina
Client: His Highness the Aga Khan
Location: Sardegna, Italy
Date: 1975
Presentation: Pencil on vellum, rendered prints
Budget: $60 million
Status: Completed

These tilt-up drawings were derived from aerial views and addressed the community's concerns regarding the imposition of the marina and the associated facilities on the existing view of the Mediterranean Sea. The drawings delineate clearly the function of the architecture, and the character of the indigenous open areas. The drawings also illustrate the flexibility of the marina itself, which accommodates vessels ranging in size from twenty feet to over three hundred feet.

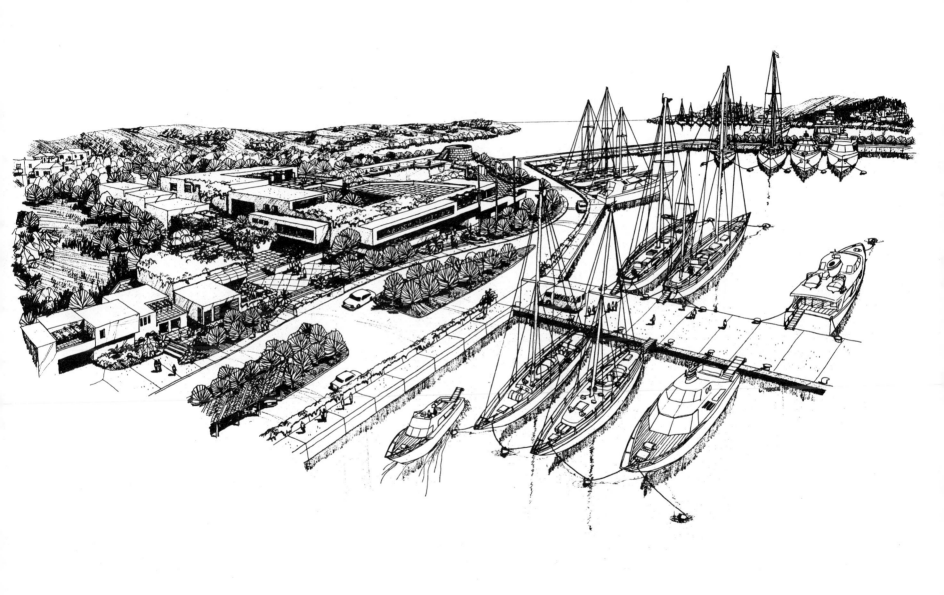

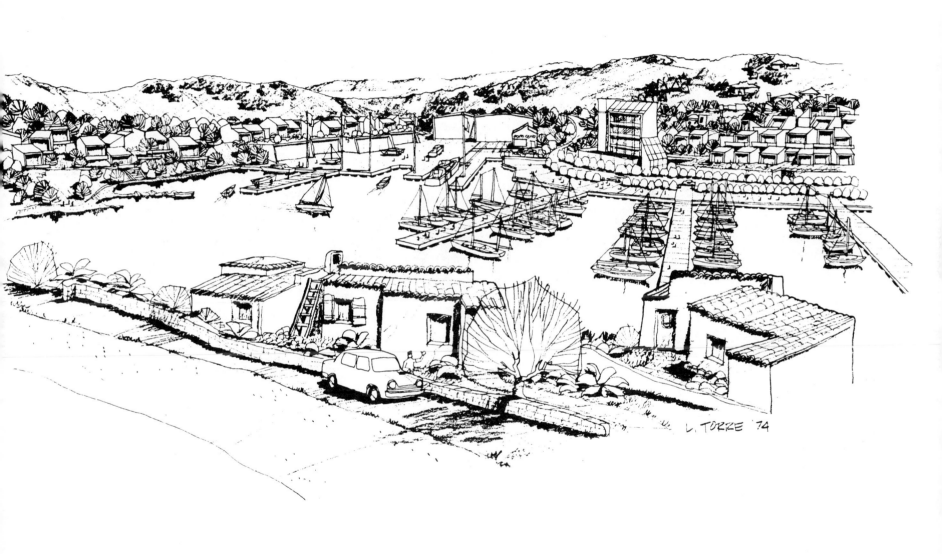

URBAN DESIGN

Project: Downtown Development District
Client: Downtown Development District
Location: Central Business District, New Orleans
Date: 1984
Presentation: Colored cibachromes
Budget: $6 million
Status: Built (installed)

This drawing of New Orleans's central business district, winner of a 1982 ASLA award, illustrates the city's transportation facilities and significant architectural and/or historical monuments. The project was predicated on the need to advertise the rejuvenation of the blighted downtown area. The drawing was used to educate and inform the public of the wealth of activities and opportunities available to them in the central business district. The tilt-up's three-dimensional quality facilitated the identification of architectural landmarks, new shopping areas, cultural centers, and the like. This drawing served as the basis for a color-coded, informational map that was installed in kiosks throughout the central business district.

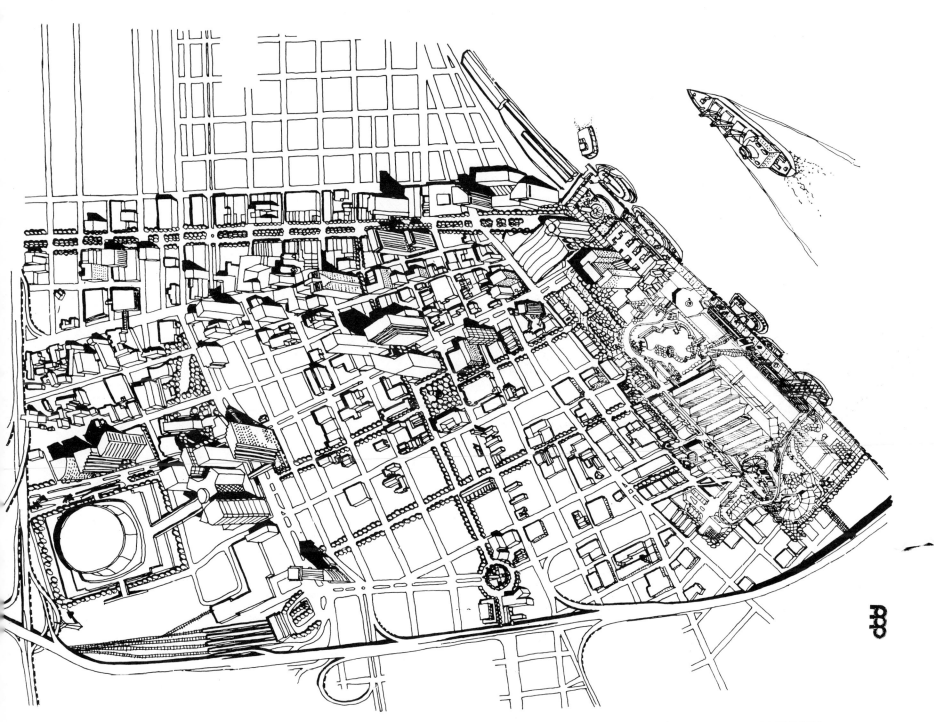

Project: St. Charles Streetscape Improvements
Client: Downtown Development District
Location: New Orleans, Louisiana
Date: 1983–84
Presentation: Promotional brochure; blackline with markers
Budget: $7 million
Status: Built

The St. Charles Street project was awarded to Design Consortium, Ltd. through a competition. Competitions allow very little time to form design concepts and to delineate a complex series of sketches that illustrate these ideas. St. Charles Street, a linear streetscape project, was one of the first tilt-ups ever done. It actually "peeled back" building facades to delineate clearly the proposed improvements to the street as well as the effects of these improvements on existing adjacent structures. The focal point of the proposal was a large glass gallery—a corridor that connected two major buildings and housed specialty retail shops, cafes, restaurants, and the like—that became the main anchor of pedestrian activity. The specific plan for the gallery and the clarity of the overall project, as well as a careful consideration of the owners and users of the area, contributed to the awarding and success of the project.

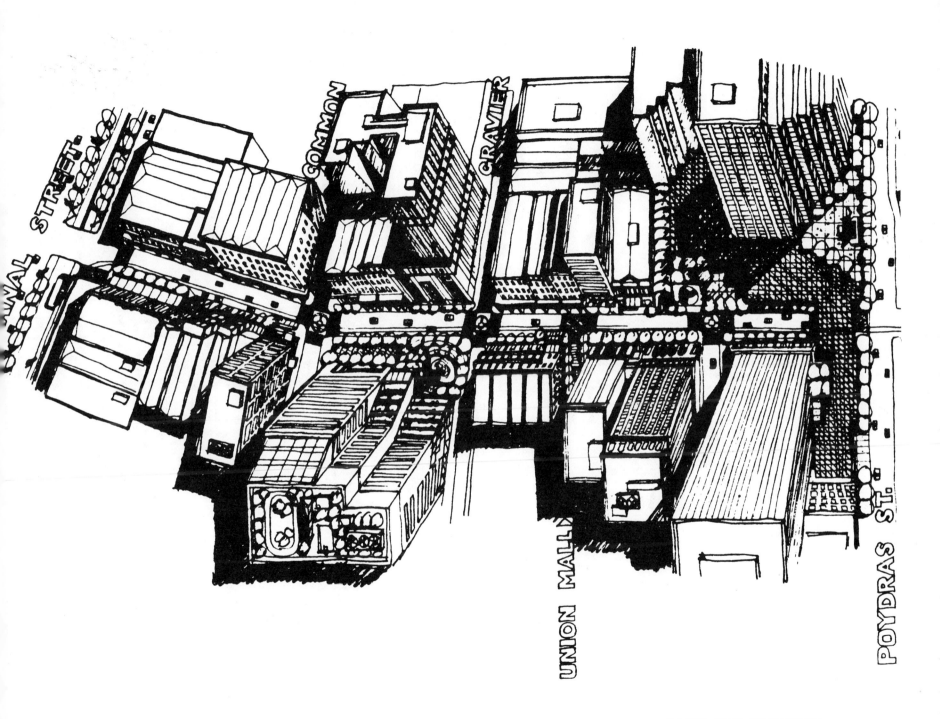

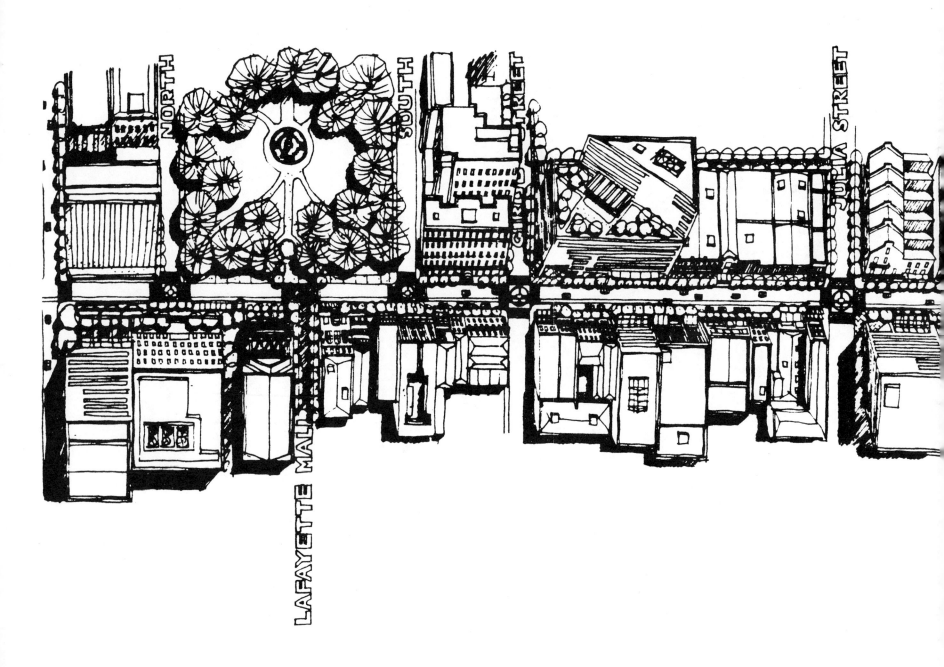

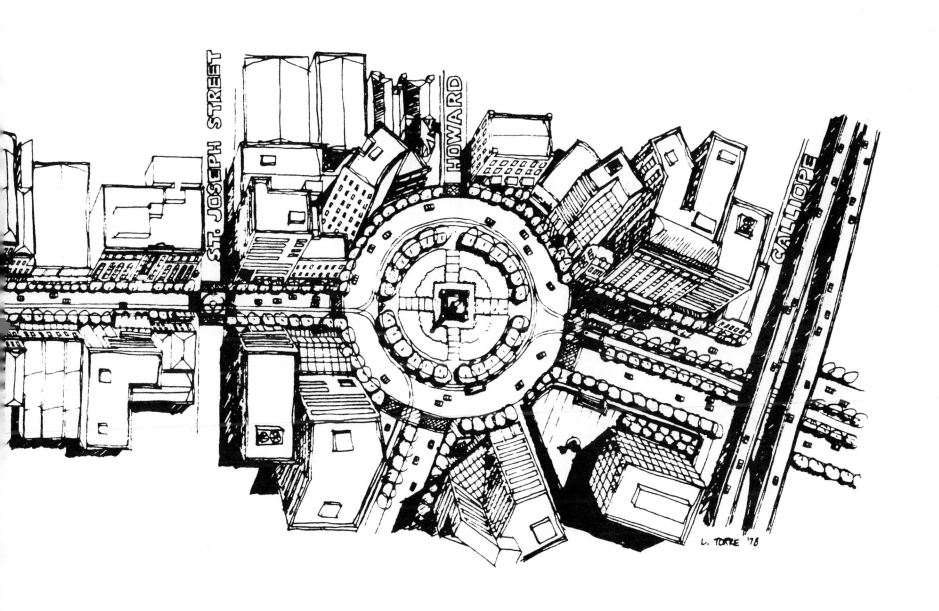

ST. JOSEPH STREET

HOWARD

CALLIOPE

L. TORRE '78

Project: Commercial Street—Natchez Mall
Client: City of New Orleans
Location: New Orleans, Louisiana
Date: 1977
Presentation: Blackline in color
Budget: $10 million
Status: In planning stages

The Union Commercial Natchez Mall, which runs through the center of the city fabric, is, like the St. Charles project, a complex urban/pedestrian project. At the time of this drawing, very few of the proposed large-scale buildings were in place. The drawing reflected the existing structures and proposed new structures in view of acceptable floor/area ratios. The drawing presented a design concept based on the future impact of these structures.

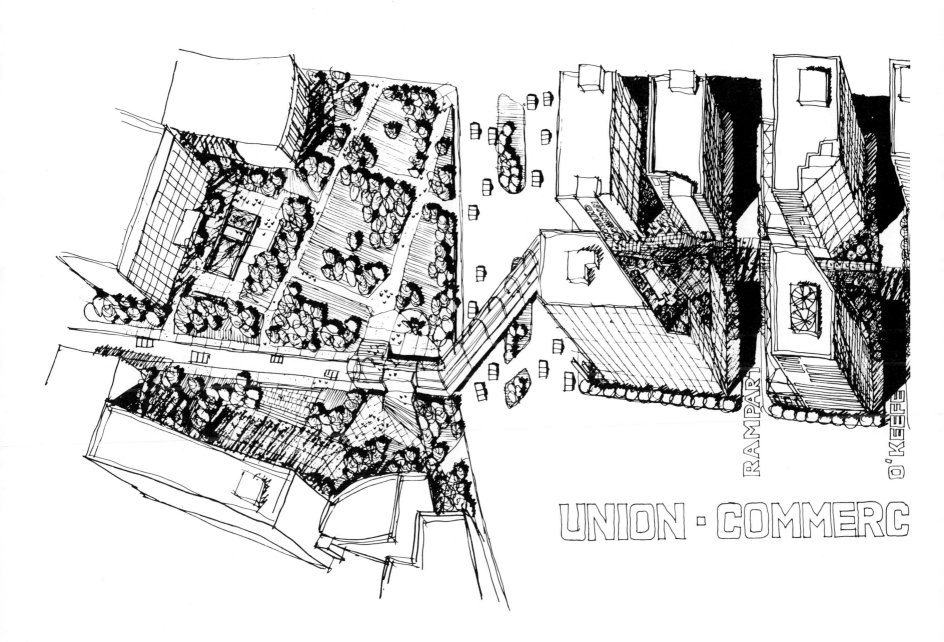

RAMPART

O'KEEFE

UNION · COMMERC

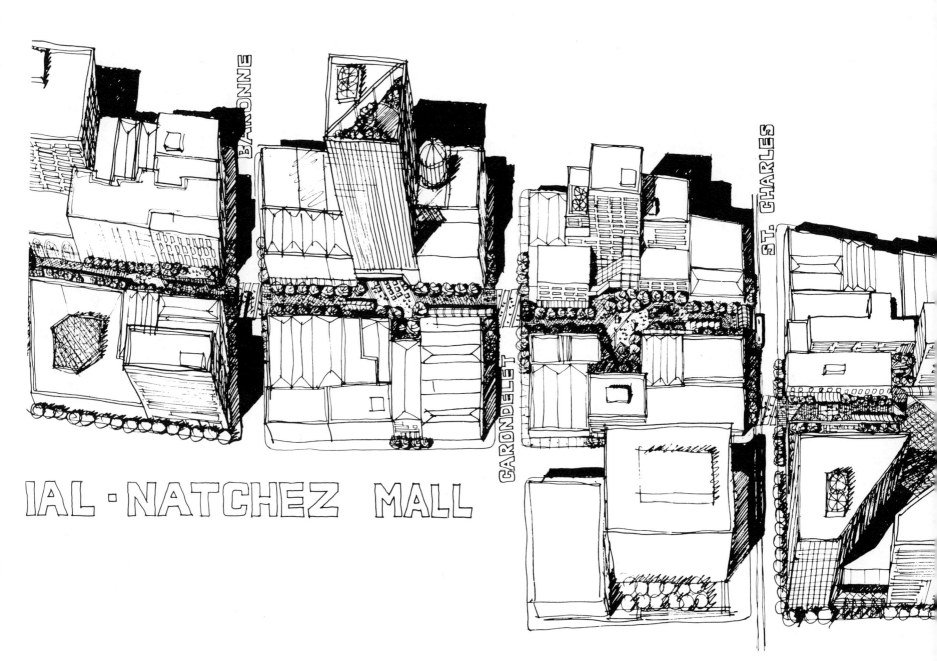

IAL · NATCHEZ MALL

BAYONNE

CARONDELET

ST. CHARLES

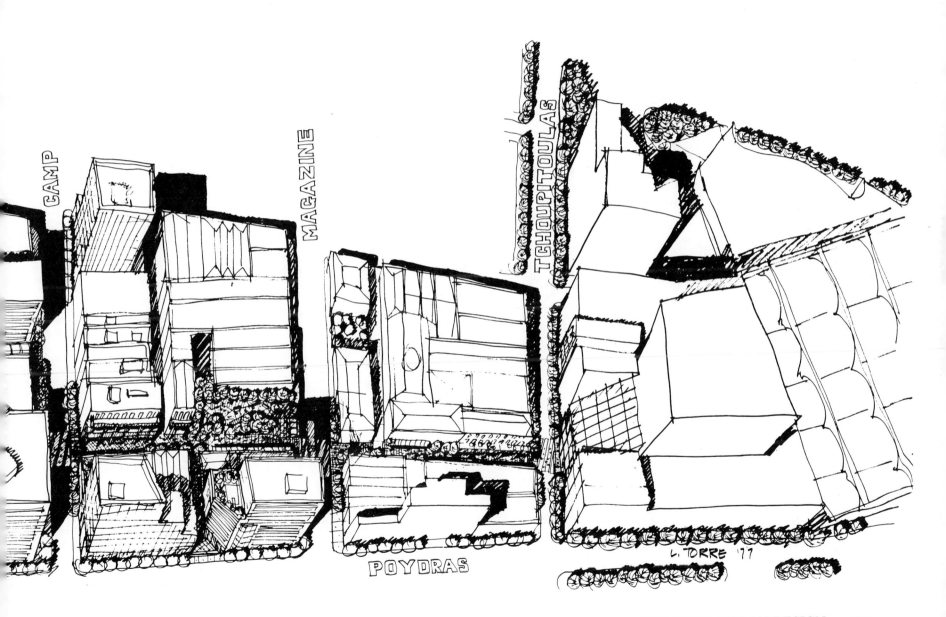

CAMP

MAGAZINE

TCHOUPITOULAS

POYDRAS

L. TORRE '77

Project:	Audubon Park Entrance
Client:	City of New Orleans, Audubon Park Commission
Location:	New Orleans, Louisiana
Date:	1984
Presentation:	Rendered blackline
Budget:	$200,000
Status:	Under construction

This project was based on an effort to recapture the original intent of the Olmsted Brothers' plan for the main entrance to the Audubon Park, situated along St. Charles Avenue. The entry pylons, symbolic balustrade, and fountain already existed, and, by adding brick pavers, the traffic flow and circulation patterns can be improved and a sense of entry created.

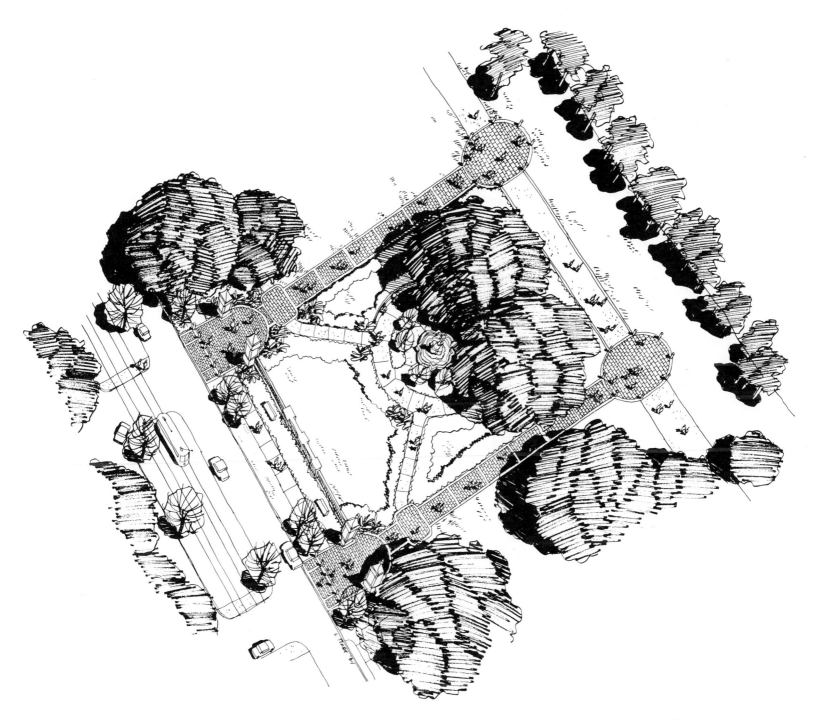

Project:	University of New Orleans Master Plan
Client:	University of New Orleans
Location:	New Orleans, Louisiana
Date:	1982
Presentation:	Blackline
Budget:	$1 million
Status:	In progress

These drawings were part of a master plan for a large community campus that has experienced rapid growth in a relatively short period of time. The site offered no distinctive features, and many existing buildings were constructed with little regard to a comprehensive plan for the area. These sketches were drawn on the basis of slides of existing conditions and were then "built up" through a series of overlays. This layering process began with a rough draft. A tracing paper overlay, on which refinements were made, was then added. A third level, also drawn on an overlay, served as the final product. The project itself is being implemented by the University of New Orleans's maintenance department.

L. TORRE '81

Project:	Holiday Inn Crowne Plaza
Client:	Holiday Inn
Location:	New Orleans, Louisiana
Date:	1983
Presentation:	Blackline
Budget:	$200,000
Status:	Built
Associated Professionals:	DMJM, Architects

The object of these proposals was to demonstrate how leftover space on a rooftop can easily be converted into usable spaces such as gardens or patios. The tilt-ups were used to illustrate the gardens in context with the existing architecture, the views from various suites in the hotel, and the flow of pedestrians in and around the area.

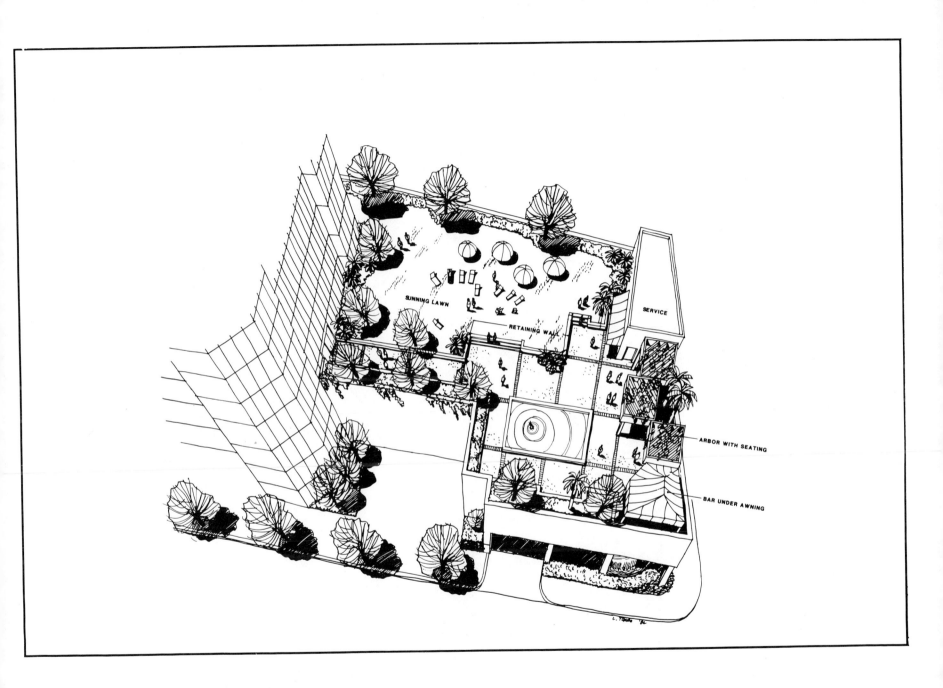

SUNNING LAWN

RETAINING WALL

SERVICE

ARBOR WITH SEATING

BAR UNDER AWNING

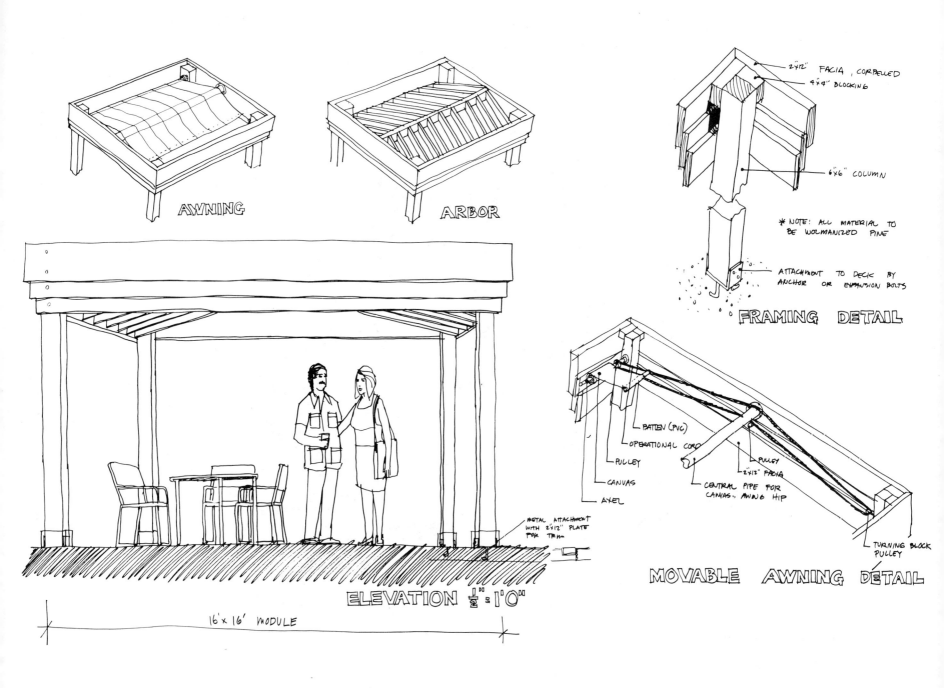

AWNING

ARBOR

2"x12" FACIA, CORBELLED

4"x4" BLOCKING

6"x6" COLUMN

* NOTE: ALL MATERIAL TO
BE WOLMANIZED PINE

ATTACHMENT TO DECK BY
ANCHOR OR EXPANSION BOLTS

FRAMING DETAIL

BATTEN (PVC)

OPERATIONAL CORD

PULLEY

CANVAS

AXEL

PULLEY

2"x12" FACIA

CENTRAL PIPE FOR
CANVAS: AWNING HIP

TURNING BLOCK
PULLEY

MOVABLE AWNING DETAIL

METAL ATTACHMENT
WITH 2"x12" PLATE
FOR TRIM

ELEVATION ½" = 1'0"

16'x16' MODULE

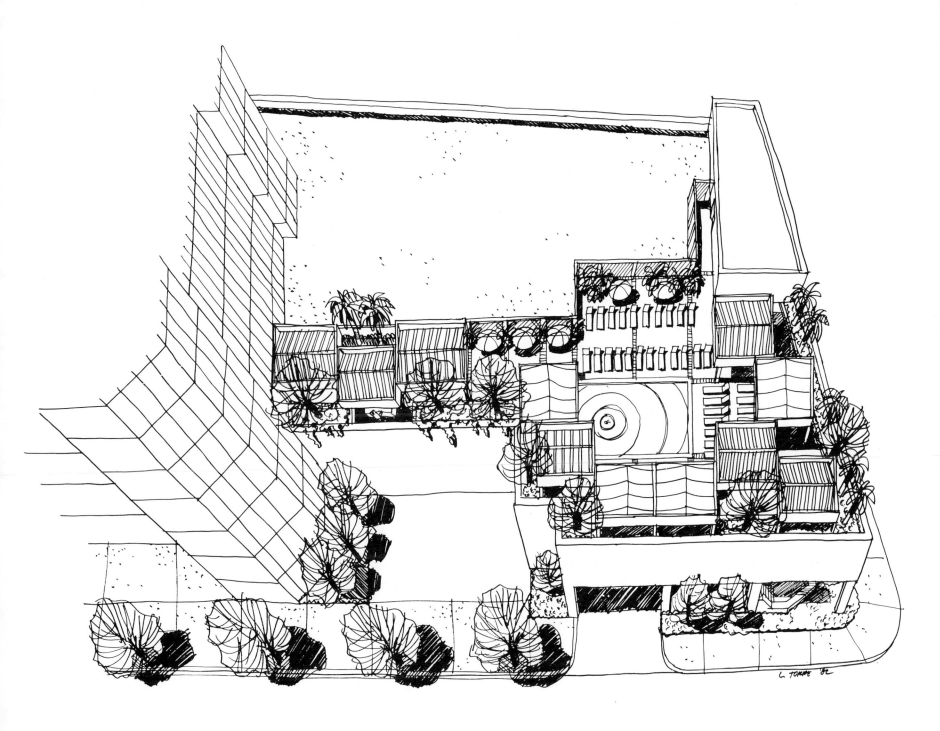

Project:	Southdown Oaks
Client:	David Elmore
Location:	Houma, Louisiana
Date:	1982
Presentation:	Blackline
Budget:	$1 million
Status:	Built

Southdown Oaks was a small office and park development project. The main objective of the design was to present a residential character. These drawings depicted successfully the project's intended architectural image by suggesting appropriate architectural scale, building materials, and the like. This enabled the owner to sell the project to prospective tenants.

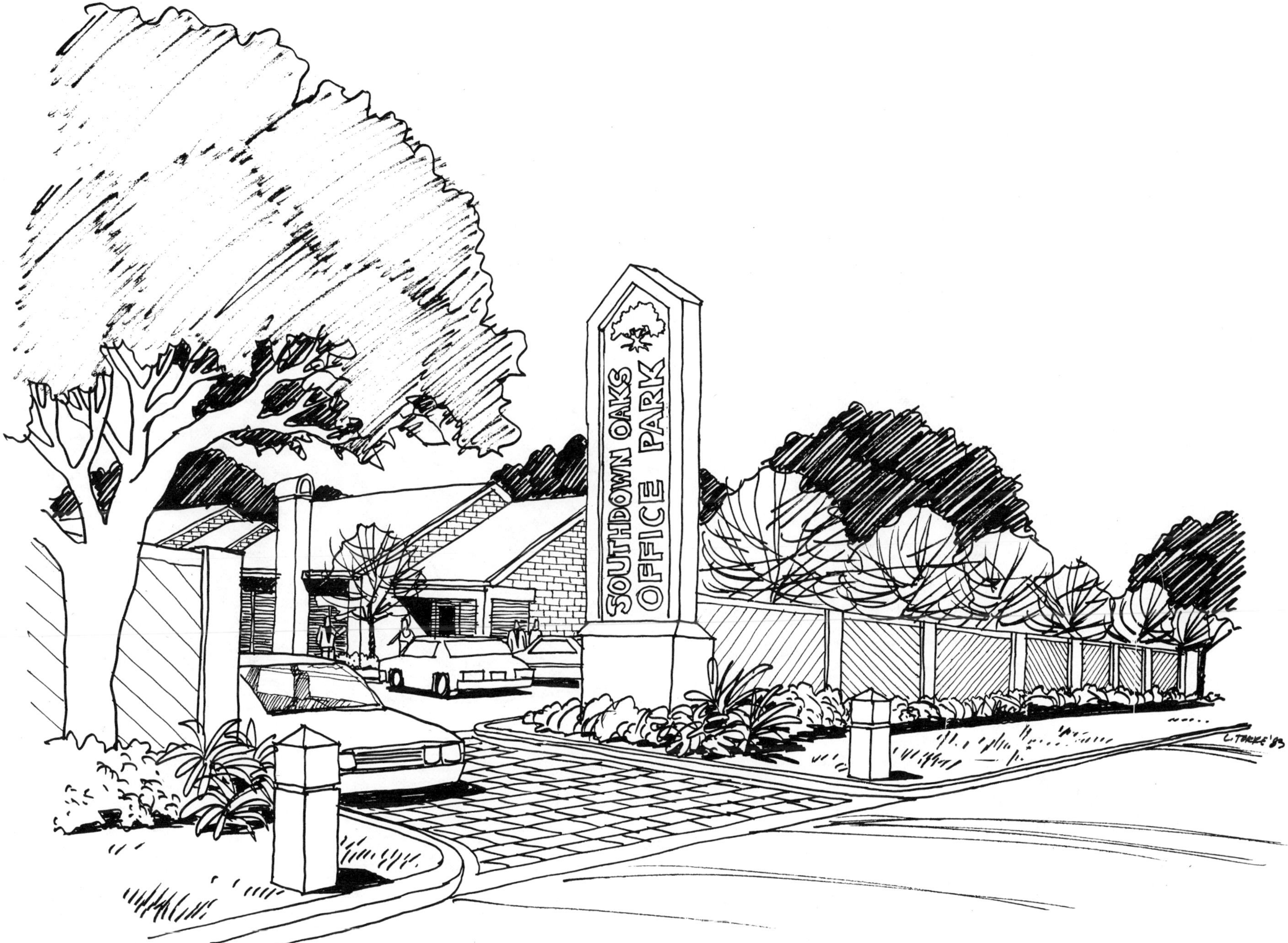
SOUTHDOWN OAKS
OFFICE PARK

Project:	Veterans Executive Office Park
Client:	J. Cannizaro
Location:	Jefferson Parish, Louisiana
Date:	1979
Presentation:	Blackline
Budget:	$100 million
Status:	Not built

This project was to be an office building/corporate headquarters complex. The drawing was used to study building massing on the 24-acre site along a major commercial corridor in Jefferson Parish, a suburb of New Orleans. It was used to suggest the arrangement of and relationship between the buildings, planting schemes, roadways, and the like.

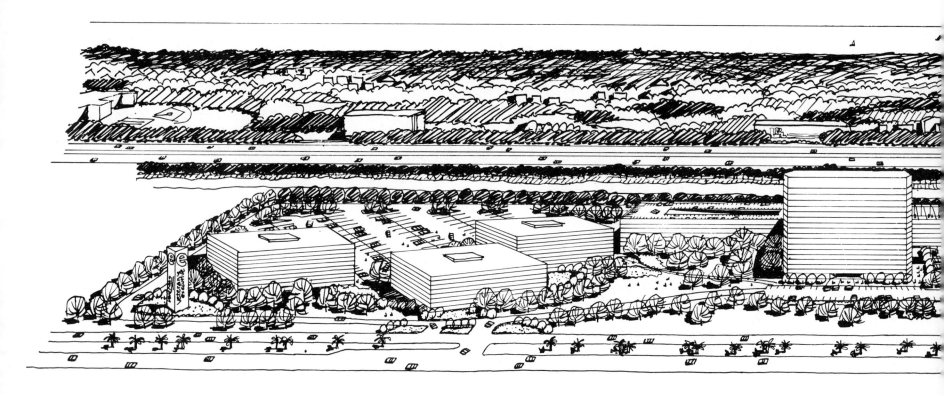

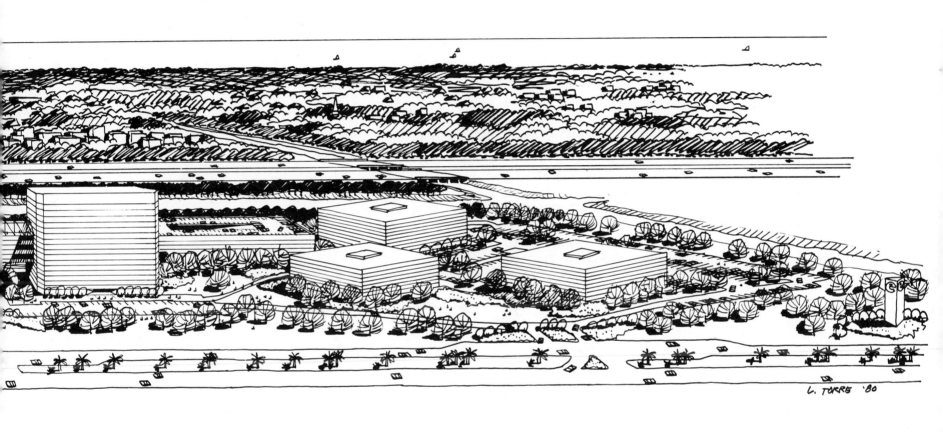

L. TORRE '80

Project:	Cafe Banquette
Client:	Moran's Riverside Restaurant
Location:	Vieux Carre, New Orleans, Louisiana
Date:	1973–74
Presentation:	Blackline rendered
Budget:	$400,000
Status:	Not built

This project proposed the enclosure of a second-floor terrace of a reconstructed building in the French Market area of New Orleans. The views from the terrace to the Mississippi River and the city of New Orleans were spectacular, but the constant river breeze and the accompanying wind-chill factor made the open space unusable for approximately six months of the year The design was based on the concept of superimposing a glass box onto the building, without changing the character of the building or the site. The glass box was to be composed of structural elements that conformed to the proportions of the columns and lintels from which the building and patio were derived.

L. TORRE '78

RIVERSIDE

LAKESIDE

Project: Junior League Show House
Client: Junior League of New Orleans
Location: New Orleans, Louisiana
Date: 1984
Presentation: Reduced for brochure
Budget: $100,000
Status: Complete

Design Consortium was asked to participate in the 1984 New Orleans Junior League Show House. Rather than designing a garden, which would have required a substantial commitment of time and effort, we prepared this orientation drawing for the publicity brochure. Specific exterior spaces were shown clearly using aerial views. Regional landscaping that would correspond to the building's architectural period and physical setting was suggested.

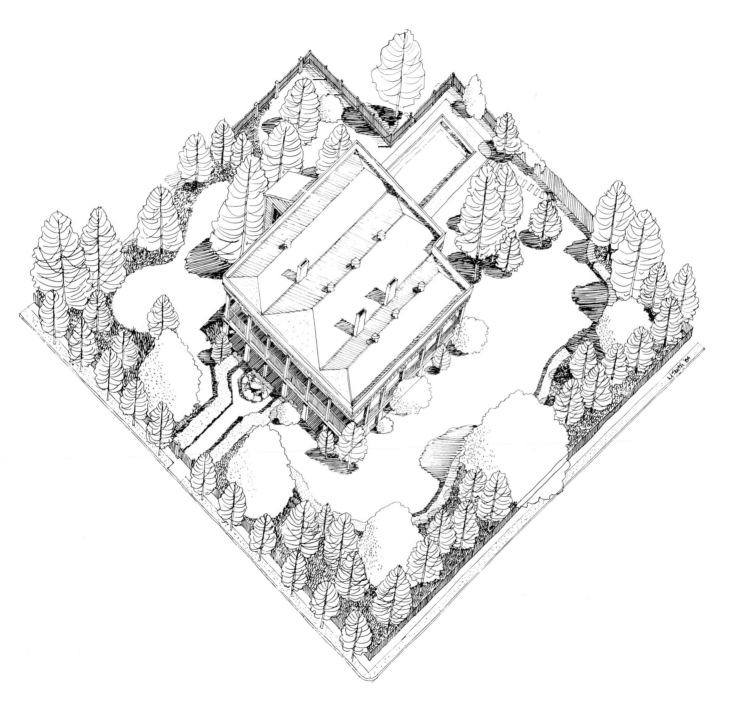

Project: Trey Yuen Restaurant
Client: T. Wong
Location: Convington, Louisiana
Date: 1982
Presentation: Blackline
Budget: $200,000
Status: Complete

The purpose of this project was to create an oriental setting for this Chinese restaurant, situated alongside a major highway. The oriental-style architecture was obviously out of character with the typical western commercial strip that runs in front of it. However, using extensive landscaping to create a buffer and isolate the building from the highway, an appropriate context was created. The drawing was effective in communicating the proposed planting schemes and landscape concepts to the client.

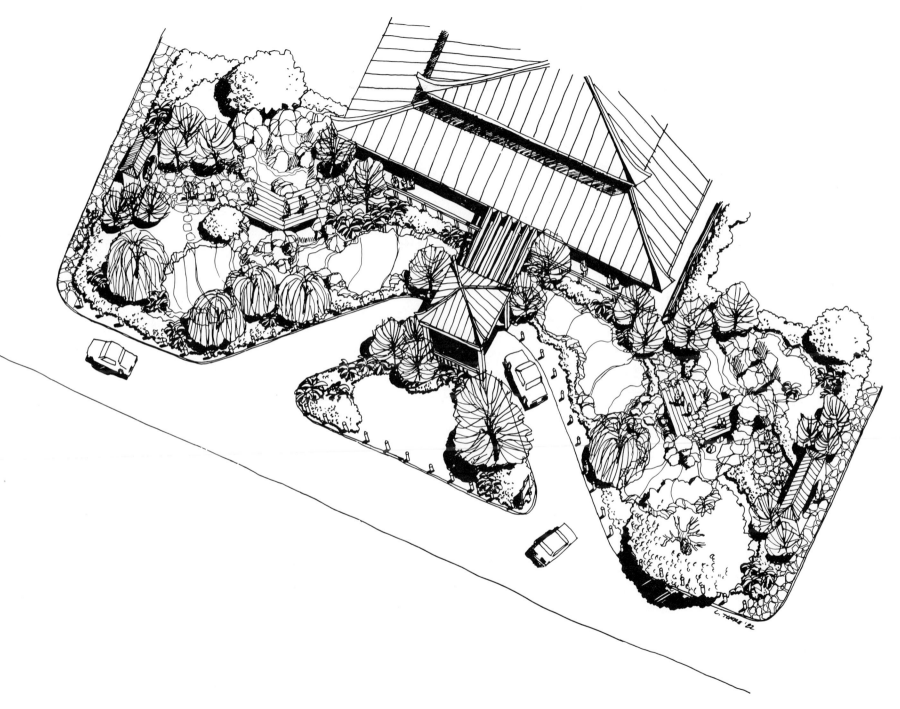

Project: Design Consortium Office
Client: Design Consortium
Location: New Orleans, Louisiana
Date: 1983
Presentation: Blackline
Budget: $200,000 total renovation
Status: Completed

In order to convert this former residence into an office building, Design Consortium had to secure the approval of neighborhood groups as well as a zoning change. The tilt-up was used to prescribe an arrangement of internal spaces that would facilitate office operations and to illustrate the proposed parking accommodations around the exterior of the building—a major concern of the neighborhood.

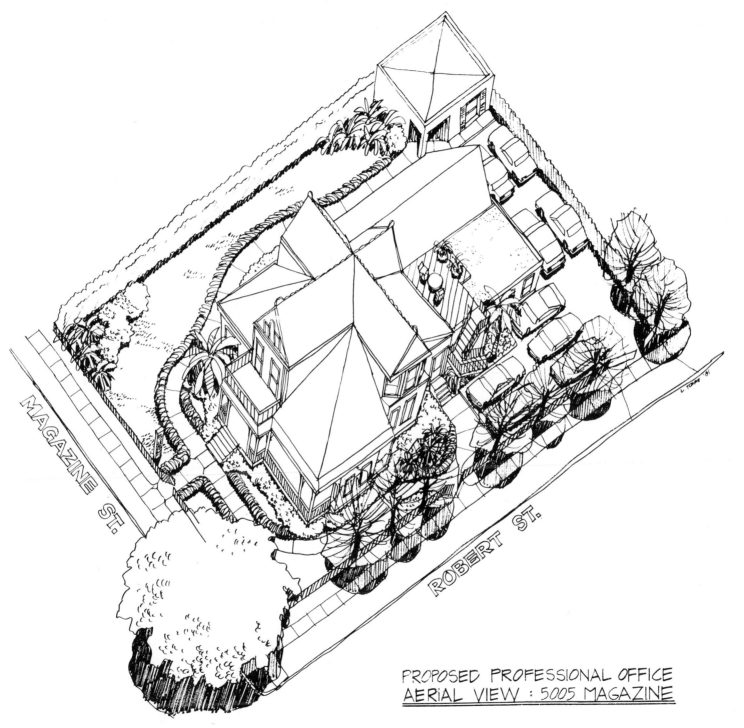

MAGAZINE ST.

ROBERT ST.

PROPOSED PROFESSIONAL OFFICE
AERIAL VIEW : 5005 MAGAZINE

COMPETITIONS

Project: Louisiana World Exposition Competition
Client: LWE, Inc.
Location: New Orleans, Louisiana
Date: 1982
Presentation: Colored blackline on presentation boards
Budget: $3 million
Status: Completed

The Louisiana World Exposition Corporation invited the submission of design proposals prior to the selection of master planners for the development. Although another design firm was ultimately selected for the master planning, Design Consortium was chosen to provide planting designs for the entire development and to design specific individual sites. For these smaller projects within the context of the total development, tilt-ups were used to define general design concepts. Detail plans were then developed from these tilt-ups.

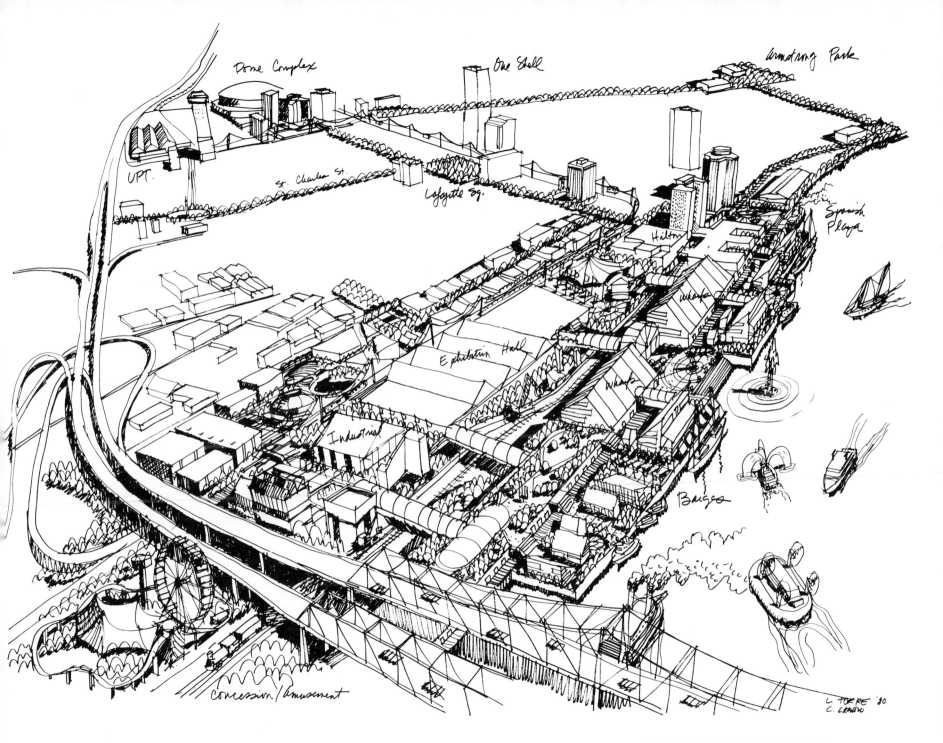

Dome Complex   One Shell   Armstrong Park

UPT.

St. Charles St.

Lafayette Sq.

Spanish Plaza

Hilton

Wharf

Exhibition Hall

Wharf

Industrial

Barges

Concession/Amusement

L. TORRE '80
C. LASRO

Project: Missoula Waterfront
Client: City of Missoula
Location: Missoula, Montana
Date: 1980
Presentation: Blackline drawings in color; aerial paste-up
Budget: $20 million
Status: Competition lost

This project was the result of a competition to design a mile-long waterfront that would provide multi-use facilities that could be used all year round. The tilt-up was used to delineate the project in its entirety, as well as focal points at each end of the site. A multi-use auditorium was at one end, and a steam bath at the other, which featured as its centerpiece, a winter garden overlooking the Missoula River plain. This scheme gave what is now the service entries of the existing buildings a new orientation toward a pedestrian mall that links the two ends of the waterfront. Steps connect the winter garden to the river promenade, under which parking space was added. The tilt-ups were done very quickly by a design team and were then developed into eye-level sketches.

ENTRY TO SHOPPING MALL

WINTER GARDEN

Text within image: MISSOULA, CITY SCAPE RESTAURANT

WINTER GARDEN RESTAURANT

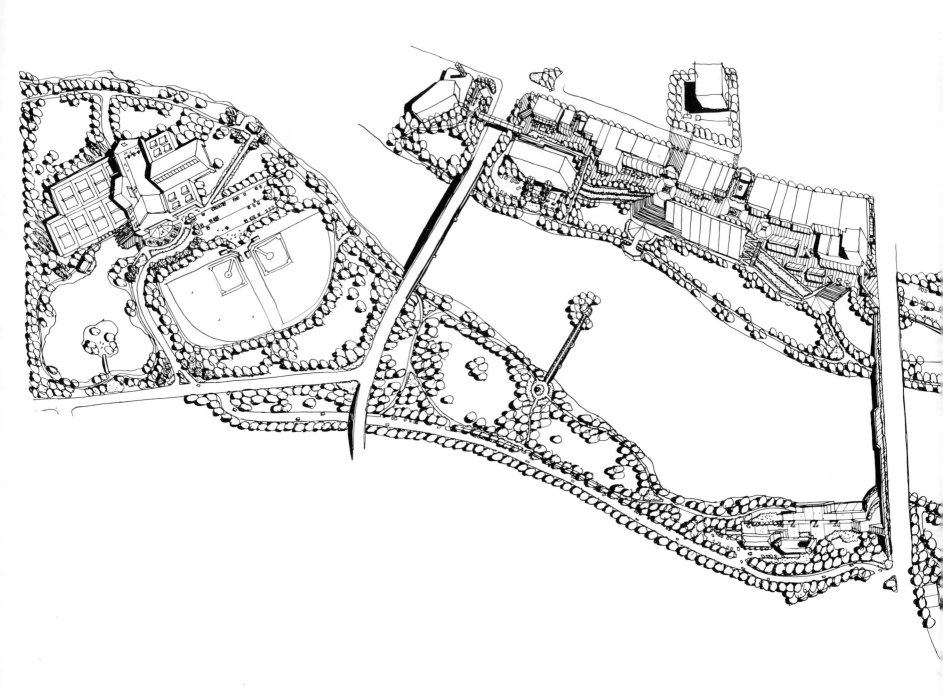

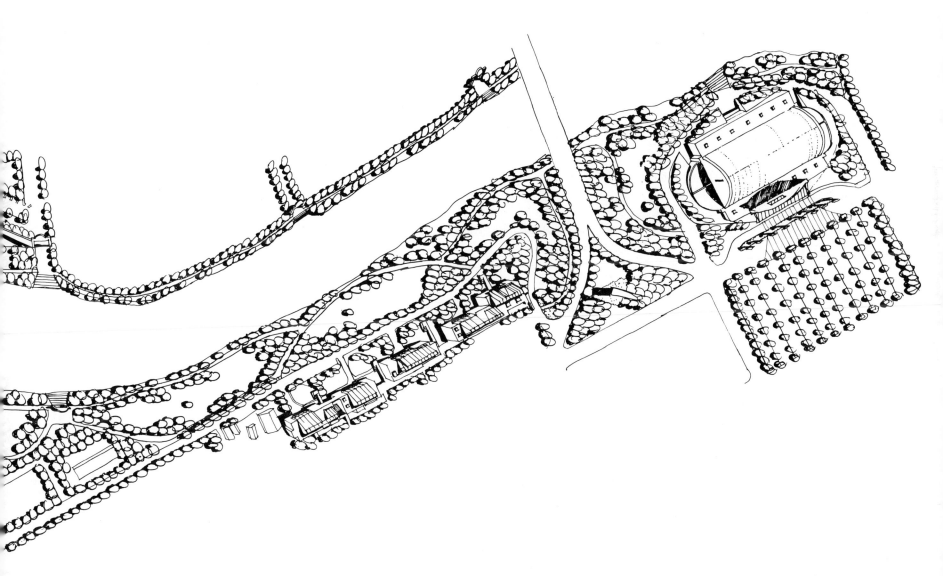

Project:	Duncan Plaza
Client:	City of New Orleans
Location:	New Orleans, Louisiana
Date:	1981
Presentation:	Blackline model
Budget:	$3.4 million
Status:	Competition won
Associated Professionals:	Robert Irwin, Sculptor

This scheme was the result of a competition sponsored by the National Endowment for the Arts in an effort to combine the talents of a sculptor (as team leader) with those of a landscape architect. The site was an open space in front of city hall. The proposal was to develop an enclosed urban aviary, with commercial facilities (restaurants, shops, and the like) interspersed with lush tropical plantings. The aviary was to become an urban branch of the Audubon Zoological Gardens. The proposal offered by Design Consortium was the unanimous choice of the jury but met with opposition in city hall due to its avant-garde use of space, and has not been built.

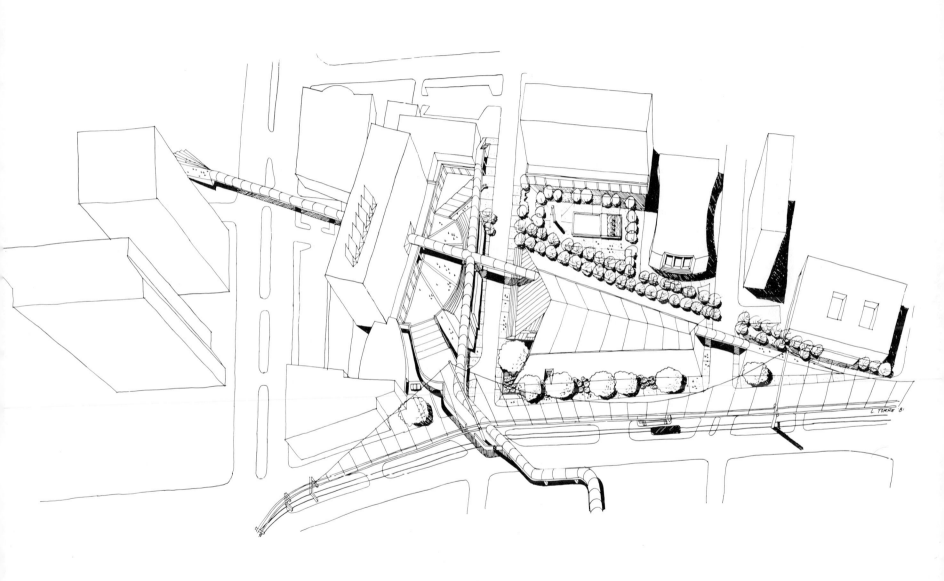

Project: Pontchartrain Beach Development
Client: Stephen Kapelow
Location: New Orleans, Louisiana
Date: 1983
Presentation: Blackline, colored
Budget: $150 million
Status: Competition lost

These drawings represent a development on the south shore of Lake Pontchartrain, on the site of an old amusement park. The plan illustrates a complex layout that provides for nine hundred units situated in clusters, with each unit maintaining a view of Lake Pontchartrain. Tilt-ups were used to show the character of the proposed residential units. Architectural scale and details, building materials, and planting schemes were selected on the basis of preserving a familiar neighborhood context and, therefore, a sense of community spirit within the development.

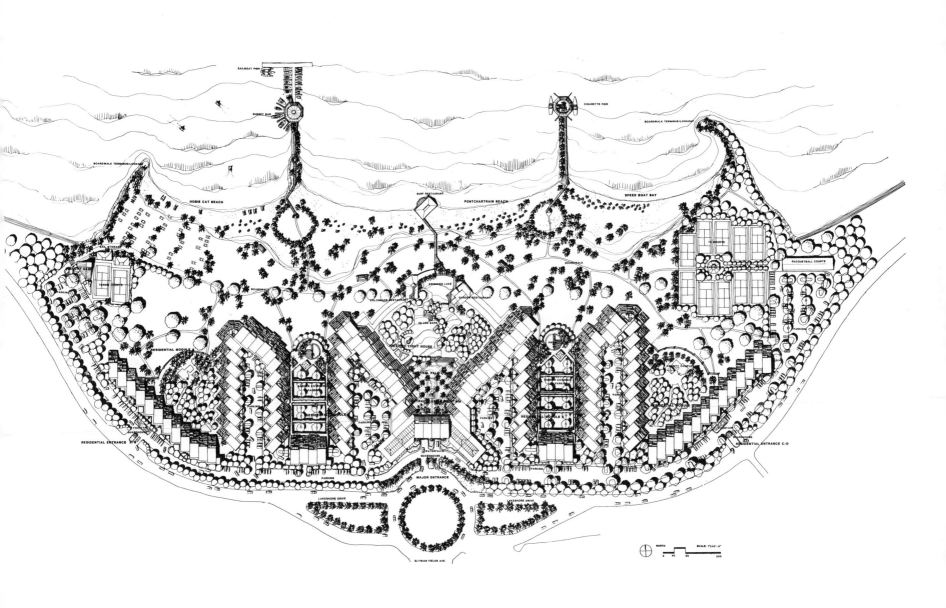

Project:	Copley Square Competition
Client:	Boston Redevelopment Authority
Location:	Boston, Massachusetts
Date:	1983
Presentation:	2 blackline
Budget:	$1 million
Status:	Merit Award

The rules and guidelines of the Copley Square competition in Boston restricted the designers to eye-level sketches and plans. We felt that this traditional plan method limited the effectiveness of our presentation since, in our opinion, the sense of scale and design of the proposal could not be tested accurately using this method. The design suggested the reiteration of the arc to create a plaza that would emanate from the building facade. This arclike pattern facilitated the linking of the square with other public areas and the more extensive city fabric.

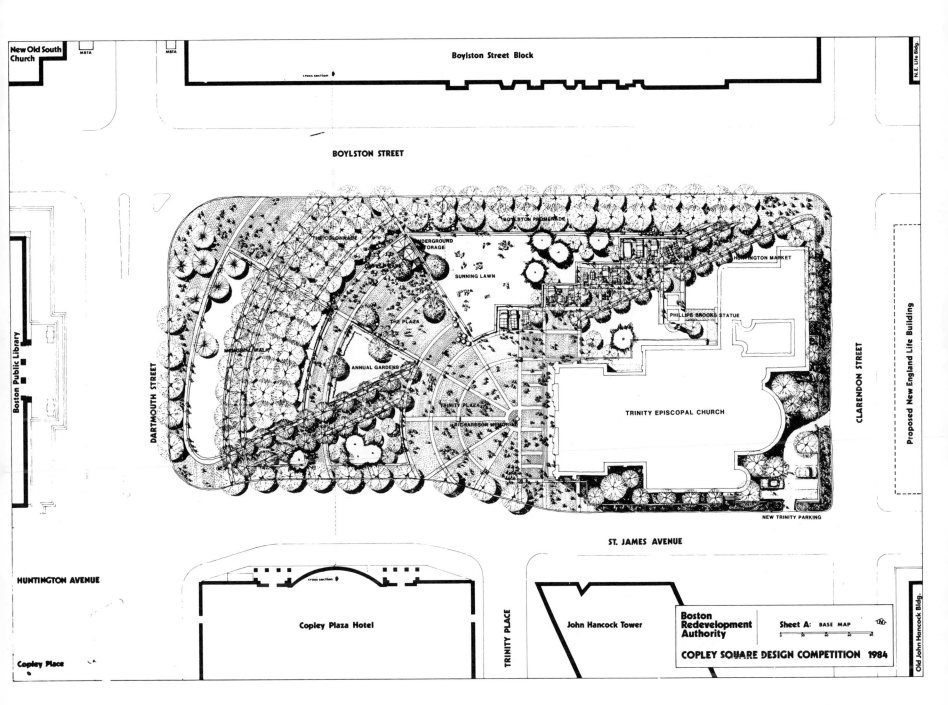

New Old South Church

MBTA   MBTA

Boylston Street Block

N.E. Life Bldg.

cross section

BOYLSTON STREET

BOYLSTON PROMENADE

THE COLONNADE

UNDERGROUND STORAGE

HUNTINGTON MARKET

SUNNING LAWN

Boston Public Library

THE PLAZA

PHILLIPS BROOKS STATUE

MEMORIAL WALK

ANNUAL GARDENS

DARTMOUTH STREET

TRINITY EPISCOPAL CHURCH

CLARENDON STREET

Proposed New England Life Building

TRINITY PLAZA

RICHARDSON MEMORIAL

NEW TRINITY PARKING

ST. JAMES AVENUE

HUNTINGTON AVENUE

cross section

Copley Plaza Hotel

TRINITY PLACE

John Hancock Tower

Boston Redevelopment Authority

Sheet A: BASE MAP

Copley Place

Old John Hancock Bldg.

COPLEY SQUARE DESIGN COMPETITION 1984

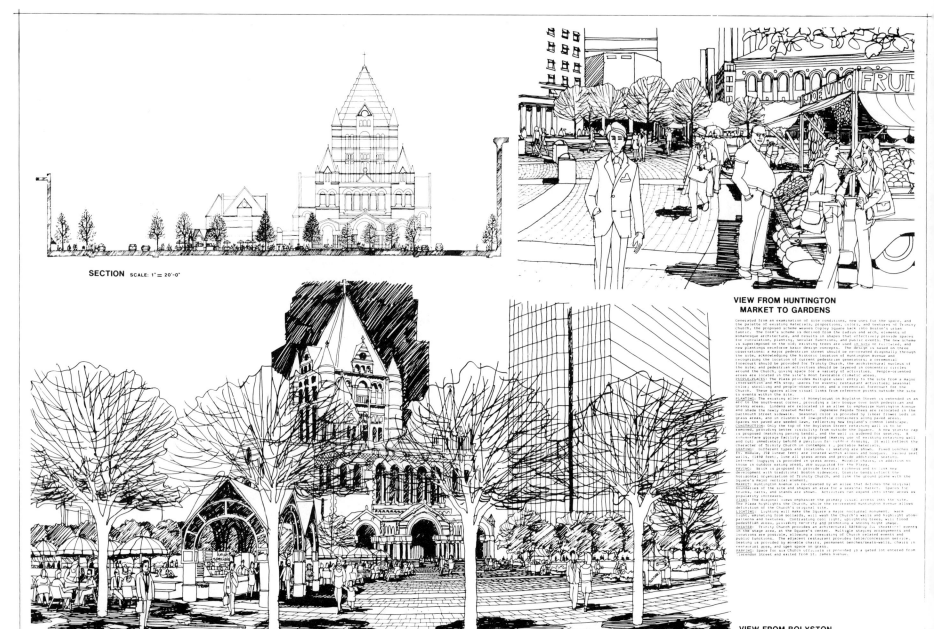

SECTION SCALE: 1" = 20'-0"

VIEW FROM HUNTINGTON MARKET TO GARDENS

Generated from an examination of site conditions, new uses for the space, and the palette of existing materials, proportions, colors, and textures of Trinity Church, the proposed scheme weaves Copley Square back into Boston's urban fabric. The form's scheme is derived from the radius and arch, elements of Romanesque architecture, and results in shapes that effectively provide spaces for circulation, planting, secular functions, and public events. The new scheme is superimposed on the old; existing trees are used in situ or re-located, and new plantings reinforce basic design concepts. The design is based on three observations: a major pedestrian street should be re-created diagonally through the site, acknowledging the historic location of Huntington Avenue and recognizing the location of current pedestrian generators; a ceremonial forecourt should be provided for Trinity Church, the architectural nucleus of the site; and pedestrian activities should be layered in concentric circles around the Church, giving space for a variety of activities. People-oriented areas are located in the site's most favorable climatic areas.

PEOPLE-PLACES: The Plaza provides multiple uses: entry to the site from a major intersection and MTA stop; spaces for events; restaurant activities; seasonal color; strolling and people-observation; and a ceremonial forecourt for the Church. These spaces allow visual links from reference points outside the site to events within the site.

PLANTING: The existing allee of honeylocust on Boylston Street is extended in an arc to the southeast corner, providing a lace bosque over both pedestrian and grassy areas. Lindens are relocated in an allee to emphasize Huntington Avenue and shade the newly created Market. Japanese Pagoda Trees are relocated on the Dartmouth Street sidewalk. Seasonal color is provided by linear flower beds in grass areas, and in clusters of low-profile containers along paved areas. Spaces not paved are seeded lawn, reflecting New England's common landscape.

CONSTRUCTION: Only the top of the Boylston Street retaining wall is to be removed, providing better visibility from outside the Square. A new granite cap is proposed (matching paving bands), and the wall is widened for seating. A subsurface storage facility is proposed (making use of existing retaining wall and cut) immediately behind a pavilion (e.g. outdoor dining). It will reflect the character of Trinity Church in contemporary, portable materials.

SEATING: Different types and locations of seating are shown. Fixed benches (20 ft. module, 150 lineal feet) are located within allees and bosques. Raised seat walls, (1490 feet), line all grass areas and provide additional seating. Informal lounging is provided in grass areas. Movable chairs, in addition to those in outdoor eating areas, are available for the Plaza.

PAVING: Brick is proposed to provide textural richness and to link new development with traditional Boston sidewalks. Granite bands reflect the horizontal organization of Trinity Church, and link the ground plane with the Square's major vertical element.

MARKET: Huntington Avenue is re-created by an allee that defines the original boundaries of the site and shapes an area for a seasonal Market. Spaces for trucks, carts, and stands are shown. Activities can expand into other areas as popularity increases.

VIEWS: The diagonal views emphasize the primary visual access into the site. The Plaza highlights the Church, while the re-created Huntington Avenue allows definition of the Church's original site.

LIGHTING: Lighting will make the Square a major nocturnal monument. Warm light, emanating from bollards, will wash the Church's walls and high light stone patterns and textures. Contrasting cool light, uplighting trees, will flood pedestrian areas, providing serenity and promoting a strong night image.

THEATER: Trinity Church provides an architectural backdrop for theatrical events in the stage area, at the Square's center. Multiple staging arrangements and locations are possible, allowing a coexisting of Church related events and public functions. The adjacent restaurant provides table/concession service. Seating is provided by movable chairs, permanent benches/seat-walls, chairs in restaurant area, and open space on grass.

PARKING: Space for six Church officials is provided in a gated lot entered from Clarendon Street and exited from St. James Avenue.

VIEW FROM BOLYSTON THRU PLAZA TO TRINITY CHURCH

Project: Los Angeles Expo '81
Client: Los Angeles Expo '81 Commission
Location: Los Angeles, California
Date: 1978
Presentation: Blackline
Budget: $300 million
Status: Project abandoned

These sketches were part of the package developed during the preliminary planning and design stages for a Class I World's Fair, to be held on an automobile racetrack outside Los Angeles in 1981. The scheme was based on a cluster development for exhibits, concessions, and features. A central lagoon, water transportation systems, and various exhibition halls were some of the elements proposed for the site. Before the design got beyond the preliminary stages, a decision was made to forgo this event for the 1984 Olympics.

L. TORRE '77

L. TORRE '77

ABOUT CASHIO · COCHRAN · TORRE/DESIGN CONSORTIUM, LTD.

Cashio • Cochran • Torre/Design Consortium staff.
Left to right: Lake Douglas, Luis Guevara, Carlos Cashio, M.E.
O'Donovan, Regina Torre, Jeffery Borchardt, Anne Calkins, Avery
Bohlke, Tom Bulloch, Alejandro Mena, Roddy Caire, Ace Torre, Jack
Cochran.

Cashio • Cochran • Torre/Design Consortium, Ltd. is a multidisciplinary landscape architecture and planning firm in New Orleans. Since its inception in 1969, the firm has been responsible for much of the award-winning landscape architecture and urban design projects in New Orleans and the Gulf South.

In the early 1970s, Design Consortium, Ltd. was selected to design the renovation of Jackson Square in the historic Vieux Carre in New Orleans, and to coordinate the reorganization of the transportation patterns in the French Quarter. These projects represented the first steps in the city's massive effort to renovate the oldest part of New Orleans, making accommodations for pedestrian activities, open spaces, and commercial developments. With the design and construction of the Jackson Square Mall, the Washington Artillery Park, the Moonwalk along the Mississippi River, the renovation of the French Market commercial complex, and the design of Edison Park, the firm developed an expertise in working with complicated issues, providing contemporary solutions within the context of the city's historical fabric. These riverfront improvements have received local and regional recognition, and an Honor Award from the American Society of Landscape Architects in 1981.

In the mid 1970s, the firm was selected as the prime consultant for the renovation and expansion of the Audubon Park and Zoological Gardens in New Orleans. Now almost complete, the redesigned zoo has received enthusiastic support from the public and recognition from the zoological community as well. In 1981 the American Association of Zoological Park and Aquariums (AAZPA) judged the Audubon Zoo as one of the top five zoos in America because of the unique way animals are exhibited, the overall design of the 57-acre facility, and the overall use of plant material.

The Audubon Zoological Gardens received a Special Judges Award from the American Association of Nurserymen in 1983 for its innovative use of plant material. The firm received the coveted AAZPA Exhibit of the Year Award in 1985 for the Louisiana Swamp Exhibit.

In 1981, Cashio • Cochran • Torre/Design Consortium, Ltd. was selected by the Downtown Development District (an organization of property owners in the central business district of New Orleans) to plan the redevelopment of St. Charles Street and to devise an information referral system for the commercial district of New Orleans. Working with legal consultants, the office wrote an ordinance for the city council that specifies the minimum requirements for sidewalk details and streetscape improvements. This information transfer system highlights 57 visual components that define the transit system, historic buildings, boundaries, services, and facilities within the Downtown Development District. It received special recognition by the Department of Housing and Urban Development as, "the most comprehensive system that has been developed in the United States to date" and received an ASLA Merit Award in 1982.

Cashio • Cochran • Torre/Design Consortium, Ltd. was the prime consultant on landscape architecture for the 1984 Louisiana World Exposition in New Orleans. The theme—*Rivers as a Source of Life*—afforded the opportunity for the firm to combine its experience in water and recreation planning with its knowledge of local planting and design traditions.

Design Consortium, Ltd. principles Carlos Cashio, Jack Cochran, L. Azeo Torre, and Luis Guevara are all graduates of Louisiana State University. Torre was awarded the Prix de Rome in landscape architecture at the American Academy in Rome in 1974–76. The firm has actively participated in educational activities, with members lecturing at Louisiana State University's College of Design, Tulane University's School of Architecture, the University of New Orleans's School of Regional Planning, the University of Montana's School of Architecture, and the American Academy in Rome.

Site perspectives is the first comprehensive collection of drawings from the firm. Design Consortium's work has been featured in various journals *(Landscape Architecture Magazine, AIA Journal, Southern Living Magazine)* and in recent books *(Yearbook of Landscape Architecture, Vol. II* and *III* [Van Nostrand Reinhold Company Inc.], and *Site Graphics* [Van Nostrand Reinhold Company Inc.]).

INDEX